Uranium

Resources Series

Peter Dauvergne & Jane Lister, *Timber*

Michael Nest, *Coltan*

Elizabeth R. DeSombre & J. Samuel Barkin, *Fish*

Jennifer Clapp, *Food, 2nd edition*

David Lewis Feldman, *Water*

Gavin Fridell, *Coffee*

Gavin Bridge & Philippe Le Billon, *Oil, 2nd edition*

Derek Hall, *Land*

Ben Richardson, *Sugar*

Ian Smillie, *Diamonds*

Adam Sneyd, *Cotton*

Bill Winders, *Grains*

Uranium

ANTHONY BURKE

polity

First published in 2017 by Polity Press

Polity Press
65 Bridge Street
Cambridge CB2 1UR, UK

Polity Press
350 Main Street
Malden, MA 02148, USA

ISBN-13: 978-0-7456-7051-5 (hardback)
ISBN-13: 978-0-7456-7052-2 (paperback)

A catalogue record for this book is available from the British Library.

Library of Congress Cataloging-in-Publication Data

Names: Burke, Anthony, 1966- author.
Title: Uranium / Anthony Burke.
Description: Cambridge, UK ; Malden, MA, USA : Polity, 2017. | Series: Resources series | Includes bibliographical references and index.
Identifiers: LCCN 2016050165 (print) | LCCN 2016051034 (ebook) | ISBN 9780745670515 (hardback) | ISBN 9780745670522 (pbk.) | ISBN 9781509510702 (Mobi) | ISBN 9781509510719 (Epub)
Subjects: LCSH: Uranium.
Classification: LCC TA480.U7 B87 2017 (print) | LCC TA480.U7 (ebook) | DDC 333.8/54932--dc23
LC record available at https://lccn.loc.gov/2016050165

Typeset in 10.5 on 13pt Scala by
Servis Filmsetting Ltd, Stockport, Cheshire
Printed and bound in the UK by Clays Ltd, St Ives PLC

For further information on Polity, visit our website:
politybooks.com.

Contents

Acknowledgements

Part of the research and writing of this book was funded by the joint UNSW–University of Birmingham project 'Nuclear ethics and global security', which is supported under the RCUK Global Uncertainties Programme – an initiative of the Economic and Social Research Council (ESRC), the Arts and Humanities Research Council (AHRC) and the Engineering and Physical Sciences Research Council (EPSRC) of the United Kingdom. I thank Catherine Edwards, Nick Wheeler and Tina Aston for their support of this project, especially for travelling to the 2015 NPT Review Conference in New York City. Polity's Louise Knight and Nekane Tanaka Galdos exhibited great patience as the delivery of this manuscript was delayed, and I am grateful for their professionalism and advice as the book was being developed. I also thank Stefanie Fishel, who read much of the final manuscript, and its reviewers, who also provided valuable advice.

Abbreviations

ABM	Anti-ballistic Missile
AEC	US Atomic Energy Commission
BMD	Ballistic Missile Defence
CDUT	Canada Deline Uranium Table
CGN	China General Nuclear Corp.
CNS	Convention on Nuclear Safety
CTBT	Comprehensive Test Ban Treaty
DGSE	Direction Générale de la Sécurité Extérieure (France)
DU	Depleted Uranium
EDF	Electricité de France (energy corp.)
EIS	Environmental Impact Assessment
EPA	Environmental Protection Agency
ERA	Energy Resources Australia
FMCT	Fissile Materials Cut-off Treaty
GWe	Gigawatt (electrical energy)
HEU	Highly Enriched Uranium
HLW	High Level Waste
HRI	Hydro Resources Inc.
IAEA	International Atomic Energy Agency
ICBM	Intercontinental Ballistic Missile
ICNND	International Commission on Nuclear Non-Proliferation and Disarmament
ILW	Intermediate Level Waste
IRBM	Intermediate-range Ballistic Missile
INES	International Nuclear and Radiological Event Scale

ISL	In-situ Leaching
LEU	Low-enriched Uranium
MIRV	Multiple Independently Targeted Re-entry Vehicle
MRBM	Medium-range Ballistic Missile
NRC	Nuclear Regulatory Commission
PER	Public Environment Report
PHS	Public Health Service (US)
METI	Ministry of Economy, Trade and Industry (Japan)
MWe	Megawatt (electrical energy)
NATO	North Atlantic Treaty Organization
NGO	Non-government Organization
NISA	Nuclear and Industrial Safety Agency (Japan)
NKVD	The People's Commissariat for Internal Affairs (USSR)
NPT	Treaty on the Nonproliferation of Nuclear Weapons
NNWS	Nonnuclear Weapons States (members of the NPT)
NSG	Nuclear Suppliers Group
NWS	Nuclear Weapons States (members of the NPT)
OEWG	Open-Ended Working Group On Taking Forward Multilateral Nuclear Disarmament Negotiations
SAC	US Strategic Air Command
SDI	Strategic Defense Initiative
SIOP	Single Integrated Operations Plan (US nuclear war plan)
SLBM	Submarine Launched Ballistic Missile
START	Strategic Arms Reduction Treaty
TEPCO	Tokyo Electric Power Company
TNT	2,4,6-trinitrotoluene
TNW	Theatre Nuclear Weapon
UN	United Nations
USSR	Union of Soviet Socialist Republics (Soviet Union)
UNC	United Nuclear Corporation
VCA	Vanadium Corporation of America
WNA	World Nuclear Association

CHAPTER ONE

The Politics of Uranium

The names Hiroshima and Fukushima have a sinister rhyme. When considered together, they are stark historical bookends to Japan's tragic experience of nuclear energy since 1945: at Hiroshima, one of only two explosions of a nuclear weapon in warfare and, at the Fukushima Daiichi power plant, the second worst nuclear accident in modern history. Two generations of Japanese, separated by half a century, had experienced the most feared outcomes of the military and industrial exploitation of a dull grey ore: uranium. This substance – whose atomic qualities enabled scientists to unlock the reactions that power the stars – has changed, secured and threatened the world and continues to reverberate through its geopolitics.

As the heaviest (and most atomically unstable) naturally occurring chemical element on earth, uranium has won a unique place in the global politics of resources. Highly enriched shells of this metal sit inside the nose cones of tens of thousands of nuclear weapons, promising enormous destruction and mortality should they ever be used. Formed into rods, it sits inside more than 430 electric power stations around the world, partially fulfilling a promise to unlock plentiful sources of energy for peaceful use by humankind, while opening up new dilemmas of nuclear safety, proliferation, terrorism and disposal. In other applications, the fission of uranium is used to create a range of radioactive substances used in medical imaging and treatment, while one of its fission products – plutonium – is used both in nuclear weapons and to power interplanetary spacecraft. In short, uranium is powerful and ironic. Put into the hands of doctors, scientists, technicians, soldiers and strategists, uranium saves lives and provides security, at the same time as it imperils human life and security on a planetary scale.

Uranium is controversial even before it is put to use in energy, military and medical applications. Protest movements, court cases, national inquiries and international treaties have been fuelled by the environmental impact of its mining, the safety and health challenges for mine workers, the costs to indigenous communities and the security implications of its sale and export. These costs, wrongs and conflict triggers are absent from the nuclear non-proliferation regime – the structure of global governance designed to control nuclear dangers – yet are no less central to the politics of this extraordinary mineral. From the time uranium was first identified as a crucial military resource, its strategic importance has driven national efforts to find it, exploit it and control it – especially to control its use, production and trade.

This book focuses on these struggles around the production, acquisition, enrichment and control of uranium as a resource, while also expanding to consider the ways it has had a major impact on the global geopolitics, and governance, of energy and security. These two levels of struggle are in fact tightly interlinked: desires for national security through nuclear weapons drove the first phases of uranium exploitation and trade; then, with the 'Atoms for Peace' programme and the ensuing growth of the nuclear power industry, nuclear energy took over as a major driver of demand. The potential for the diversion of highly enriched uranium from peaceful to weapons use remains a major concern in the non-proliferation and 'nuclear security' regime – shaping debates around Iran's nuclear programme and the ethics of uranium sales to India, motivating calls for international control over the enrichment and sale of uranium through the establishment of an international 'fuel bank', and driving efforts to conclude a global Fissile Materials Cutoff Treaty (FMCT) to end the production of weapons-grade uranium and assist efforts to control the illegal trade in fissile materials.

Uranium is also big business. The involvement of some of the world's largest corporations in the mining, nuclear power and weapons industries has generated considerable political pressures, dangers and regulatory challenges. Nuclear energy has been touted by business lobbies (and some scientists) as a promising source of carbon-free electricity as the dangers of global climate change become the focus of governments around the world; however, the reactor meltdowns at Fukushima in 2011 have tainted this promise and renewed attention to questions of safety, regulation and disposal. It even led some countries to commit to phasing out nuclear power altogether. At the same time, fears of transnational terrorism and the long-appreciated dangers of nuclear war have led the leaderships of four major nuclear powers – the USA, UK, France and Russia – to proclaim a goal of total nuclear disarmament over the next few decades.[1] However, optimism is premature. This goal not only creates complex new strategic and regulatory challenges; it occurs amid new political and proliferation pressures that may render the disarmament enterprise stillborn.

Uranium: a strategic substance

Uranium is a metal and a pure chemical element – that is, one of the fundamental units of matter, listed in the Periodic Table of Elements. A chemical element is a substance containing a single type of atom and the periodic table lists them in ascending order of atomic number – the number of protons in the nucleus. Uranium is high on the periodic table, having an atomic number of 92 in its naturally occurring form, causing it to decay naturally into other elements over time. This decay is termed radioactivity and is what made uranium especially attractive to physicists seeking to investigate atomic structures and induce nuclear fission. Uranium is also naturally abundant in comparison to its other 'heavy' radioactive cousins, many of which are only present in trace quantities. It is as common in the earth's crust as zinc or tin and is present in much smaller concentrations in most rocks and in the oceans. It was these fundamental chemical qualities that laid the ground for uranium's strategic and world-transforming importance, when the obscure investigations of quantum physicists merged, in the 1930s and 1940s, with the ambitions and insecurities of states and the cascade into global war.

It is sobering to consider that, aside from the final days of the Allied war with Japan, uranium weapons were not used in the Second World War and instead shaped the cultural, strategic and political architecture of the Cold War and beyond. In fact the bombings of Nagasaki and Hiroshima have been referred to as the opening blows of the Cold War, given that they were used there as much to intimidate the Soviet Union and preclude it from the occupation of Japan as to induce a rapid Japanese surrender.[2] Yet imagine the vast landscape of devastation had the weapons been available to the belligerent powers a few years earlier – which they almost were! The physicist Enrico Fermi and his Rome group successfully conducted nuclear fission in 1934 – but failed to recognize it as such – four years before the nuclear chain reaction was decisively identified in Germany, immediately triggering widespread consideration of its military implications.[3] Consider that atomic bombs were produced less than four years after the 1939 publications that confirmed nuclear fission: what would have occurred if Fermi had recognized the true import of his discovery? Might atomic bombs have been used in desperation against London, Paris and Moscow, or in

France and Poland as Allied forces surged towards Germany in 1944? Would they then have been used in retaliation? The destruction of Hiroshima and Nagasaki demonstrated that there was no 'nuclear taboo' in place at that time and showed the human and physical devastation that would occur when military exhaustion, desperation and perceptions of strategic advantage coalesced. Would the Cold War arms race then have been averted, as the world pondered the scale of the devastation, or accelerated, as they sought to outrun its next wave?

Global reserves of uranium are thought to be vast, but their economic and strategic significance depends on two issues. First, their location, which exposes particular communities to the effects of mining and competition, may fuel conflict and generate geopolitical struggles over control and access. Second is the associated cost of extraction and the uses that become available as a result. In recent decades known reserves have in fact increased because exploration, reflecting perceived market potential, has expanded. In 2011, world known reserves were 5.3 million tonnes. Australia held 1.7 million tonnes, 32 per cent of world reserves and Kazakhstan, the second largest reserve of 629,000 tonnes, 12 per cent of world totals. Other significant reserves are held in Russia (9%), Canada (9%), Niger (9%), South Africa (8%), Brazil (5%), Namibia (5%) and the USA (4%).[4] Many of these countries, especially Australia, Canada, the USA and South Africa, are settler-colonial states with bitter histories of violence, dispossession and racial inequality and many of their mines are located on (or close to) indigenous lands. This supply of terrestrial uranium is estimated to be viable for another eighty years based on current usage rates in conventional reactors, but new reserves are likely to become available if prices increase. Furthermore, technologies to extract uranium from seawater are developing, if currently uneconomic. It is estimated that the oceans contain over four billion tonnes of uranium, which could meet the entire global need for electricity for upwards of 900 years.[5]

A troubled decade

The devastating tsunamis that hit Japan on 11 March 2011 crowned a decade of global tumult and fears over the potentials of nuclear energy. The decade began with a bold series of demands for nuclear security and disarmament from the 190 members of the Treaty on the Non-Proliferation of Nuclear Weapons (NPT), saw the same 'review' conference in 2005 deteriorate into a brutal stalemate without progress, and concluded with nuclear tests by North Korea, frantic diplomatic efforts to forestall an Israeli attack on Iran's nuclear facilities, deadlock in the US Congress over a new strategic arms reduction treaty with Russia, and the tragedy of Fukushima. There, two tsunamis up to 15 metres in height overwhelmed the power station's protections, killing all electricity to two reactors and seriously damaging the other four. Cooling systems broke down, fuel rods melted, and three of the reactor housings exploded, releasing seventeen million curies of radiation into the air and 0.127 million curies into the sea. By 12 April the Nuclear Safety and Industrial Agency of Japan had rated the disaster a 7, a 'major accident' highest on the International Atomic Energy Agency (IAEA) International Nuclear and Radiological Event Scale (INES). This was the same rating given to the comparably more devastating accident at Chernobyl, Ukraine, in 1986. Fukushima Daiichi was the thirty-third serious accident at a nuclear power plant since 1952.[6]

Earlier in the decade, as the 2000 NPT Review Conference set out a 13-point path to global disarmament, American nuclear strategists were reviving old dreams of making nuclear weapons usable, while new concerns over the proliferation of uranium supplies and technology to 'rogue states' such as Iraq, Libya, Iran and North Korea came to the fore.[7] While Iraq proved to have abandoned its weapons programme and Libya agreed to end its efforts and open its facilities to international scrutiny, Iran and North Korea pushed on, citing concerns about their future energy and national security. The 2010 NPT Review conference then revived hopes in global nuclear disarmament and governance with a 64-point action plan, hopes that by 2016 were rapidly dissipating.

The decade also bridged important challenges to uranium miners and governments from indigenous people. In the late 1990s, the Mirarr Aboriginal tribe of Queensland's Kakadu World Heritage Area opposed plans to build a new uranium mine at Jabiluka, forcing its mothballing, while in April 2011, as the Fukushima disaster reached its full height, two Navajo communities in New Mexico presented their case against the US Nuclear Regulatory Commission's grant of a licence for two uranium mines on their lands to the Inter-American Commission on Human Rights. The Navajo, who had worked in numerous mines in the region during the Cold War, were especially conscious of the contamination of their lands and ongoing health problems such as birth defects, cancer and heart disease. Here, the demand for uranium cuts across international law, the conflict with national law over resources and land rights and the power that states have over indigenous peoples by virtue of dispossession and the legal expropriation of their lands.

This is a book about the world that uranium has helped to bring about: the discovery of its distinctive atomic properties in parallel with two world wars and the rapid development of quantum physics as a field; the global race to find, control and exploit its mineral reserves; the development and proliferation of nuclear weapons and strategic plans for their use, which has had such a dramatic effect on the landscape of global insecurity; the growth of nuclear electric power and its complicated interrelation with questions of proliferation and climate change; and the profound moral questions raised by a situation in which the very life of humanity and planet Earth have been put into peril for a few states' national security. It also looks ahead, to consider the futures of conflict, disarmament or proliferation that coming decades may bring and to consider how adequate our current thinking and regulatory systems are to cope with future nuclear dangers.

The book thus addresses both uranium and the nuclear applications, potentials and dangers its exploitation has helped to bring about, and refers to a range of related substances (such as plutonium, thorium, hydrogen and tritium) that atomic and weapons research has produced and utilized. The book is also widely concerned with the historical, social, ethical and political impacts that these substances have had, beyond the traditional concerns with energy and security. Energy and security are certainly important, but are understood too narrowly. This limits our ability to understand and appreciate how different uses and histories of the resource are linked together and the variety of challenges and wrongs with which it is associated. Debates about nuclear energy focus around electricity prices, renewable energy and climate change, but rarely touch on the ecological and social impact of uranium mining. A similar problem haunts the nuclear non-proliferation regime, which grants states a basic right to civilian uses of nuclear energy with limited international oversight and is mainly concerned with preventing the proliferation of nuclear weapons, technology and weapons-grade fissionable materials. This lack of international oversight was arguably a factor in the Fukushima tragedy. In a different way, the lingering damage to the health and human rights of indigenous peoples and other communities from nuclear testing and mining is a moral silence at the heart of the regime; it is not seen as relevant to international security.

This book is not written primarily as a theoretical or even academic work. However a theoretical strand can be traced through its overall narrative. The book is informed by a hybrid of structuralist and 'new materialist' ways of thinking about how matter and things are taken up by societies and transform them. This perspective sees matter – such as uranium – as having a raw materiality and agency that *acts on* the world, in a way that resists, frustrates and channels human intentions. Uranium is an *actant*, in Bruno Latour's terms.[8] Uranium's radioactivity, its heavy and unstable nucleus, and its ubiquity in the earth's crust, are facts that enable it to do things and make a difference. At the same time, *ideas* – formal and informal knowledges, natural and social sciences, ideologies, cultural practices, even emotions – also shape the encounter that society has with matter and especially shape how it is transformed into technology and integrated into social, economic and political systems.[9] Consider the equation that was discovered by Albert Einstein, which expresses the enormous reserves of energy contained in even small amounts of matter: $E = Mc^2$, energy equals mass times the speed of light squared. The discovery of this equation, even as it expressed an important scientific fact, was quickly absorbed into our politics and our concepts. Our ideas, our culture and our politics strongly shaped how uranium would be utilized and exploited, while its actancy often troubled and frustrated those very uses. That is why there have been such intense ethical and political controversies over technological developments associated with nuclear weapons and energy and why it is so mistaken to believe that technologies – even weapons – are neutral tools that we can wield and shape to our will. This kind of critical thinking about the relationship between ideas, science and matter has thus become influential in Science and Technology Studies.

Hence, there was nothing inevitable about the joining of

uranium and geopolitics. There was nothing inevitable about the transformation of an obscure mineral into the engine of fearsome weapons, a global electricity industry, or a problem for international law. Nor was there anything inevitable about the distinctive *ways* that uranium was transformed into these things. In a different world – one less predisposed to war and better organized to prevent conflict and control the evolution of technological systems ethically – uranium may have been used solely for medical applications. Uranium can only be used for bombs in a world where bombs and strategic theories for their use exist, such as the airpower theory of Guilio Douhet – which advocated attacking citizens and cities as the basis of enemy morale. At the birth of the nuclear age, in 1945, developed notions of nuclear deterrence did not exist; rather they evolved slowly over the next four decades, in competition with other perspectives that saw the weapons as useful in warfare.[10] Matter and society interact in complex and unpredictable ways and are not always susceptible to instrumental control. As I have argued elsewhere, the confidence of nuclear strategists that they could control and harness the awesome power of the atom for strategic purposes foundered on both the geopolitical dynamics they set into play and the unprecedented properties of atomic weapons themselves. This could happen, in part, because they forgot that there was 'a troubled universe of decisions between equation, conception, production and use'.[11]

The non-proliferation regime

The international society of states has developed a complex – and somewhat awkward – system of limiting the spread of nuclear weapons and regulating the sale, use and spread of uranium, other fissile materials and nuclear technology. It is made up of some nine major international treaties, a number of bilateral treaties between nuclear states, United Nations bodies and other subsidiary agencies, and *ad-hoc* cooperative activities by states. These treaties and agreements in turn intersect with other national and international forms of regulation of uranium mining, export and civilian nuclear energy. These include environmental and Aboriginal land rights laws that govern the approval and operation of mine projects.

This system is commonly termed the 'non-proliferation regime' and is centred on the 1968 Treaty on the Non-Proliferation of Nuclear Weapons (NPT). The treaty is based on a 'grand bargain' between states that possessed nuclear weapons prior to the treaty coming into force and those who did not. Under Article II of the treaty, Non-Nuclear Weapons States (NNWS) agreed not to receive nuclear weapons or technology from another state nor construct weapons themselves and under Article IV, all members have the 'inalienable right . . . to develop research, production and use of nuclear energy for peaceful purposes'. For their part, Nuclear Weapons States (NWS) undertook, under Article I, 'not to transfer to any recipient whatsoever nuclear weapons or other nuclear explosive devices or control over such weapons or explosive devices directly, or indirectly' or encourage a state to develop nuclear weapons. In a key part of the bargain, NWS also agreed, under Article VI, 'to pursue negotiations in good faith on effective measures relating to cessation of the nuclear arms race at an early date and to nuclear disarmament and on a treaty on general and complete disarmament under strict and effective international control'.[12]

Article VI has been a focus of tension and acrimony between the NWS and NNWS since the treaty came into force. Its wording reflected the refusal of NWS to accept any 'binding' or time-limited commitment to disarmament, or to embed in the treaty 'negative security assurances' to NNWS that they would not be targeted or attacked with nuclear weapons.[13] The 'grand bargain' (which can be boiled down to: Non-development + peaceful uses = Weapons retention + disarmament) is thus inherently unstable. The superpowers in fact dramatically proliferated their nuclear arsenals *vertically* during the 1970s and 1980s – that is, upwards in number – and the slow pace of disarmament negotiations since the end of the Cold War has grated with the non-nuclear states.[14]

The other key provision of the treaty is contained in Article III, which specifies 'safeguards' for the control of the production and use of fissile material. NNWS undertook to accept oversight from the International Atomic Energy Agency (IAEA) of all fissile production facilities 'with a view to preventing diversion of nuclear energy from peaceful uses to nuclear weapons or other nuclear explosive devices', while all states agreed not to provide fissionable materials or processing equipment 'to any non-nuclear-weapon State for peaceful purposes, unless the source or special fissionable material shall be subject to the safeguards required by this Article'. After North Korea's secret weapons programme was revealed, the IAEA Board of Governors adopted in 1997 a 'Model Additional Protocol' which grants the agency expanded rights of access to information and sites.[15]

With 190 state members, the NPT is one of the most universally ratified in the world. In this, it is one of the world's most successful security regimes, but also paradoxically vulnerable. Its tiny number of *non-members* expose dramatic weaknesses in its architecture. The Democratic People's Republic of Korea announced its withdrawal from the NPT in 2003 (effectively reducing it to 189 members) and thereby exposed a dangerous consequence of its provisions: that a member state could spend many years taking advantage of the Article IV rights to acquire nuclear technology for ostensibly peaceful purposes and then, as it passes the threshold to creating a nuclear weapon, withdraw and evade its Article II obligations 'not to manufacture or otherwise acquire nuclear weapons or other nuclear explosive devices'. North Korea has been slowly enriching uranium and has conducted five weapons tests and a number of test missile launches and is thus on a path to becoming a nuclear power – albeit one under severe pressure from the international community. The three other nuclear states – Israel, India and Pakistan – are excluded from joining the NPT as NWS because that category is limited to those states which manufactured and exploded a nuclear weapon prior to 1 January 1967. This means that they are bound legally by none of the key NPT obligations – being neither NNWS nor NWS – and can produce fissile material without being a part of the IAEA safeguards system.

This became an urgent issue once the full activities of the leading Pakistani nuclear scientist A. Q. Khan – who sold enrichment technology over a decade to North Korea, Iran and Libya and also made contact with radical Islamists – was revealed. Transfers to Iran and North Korea used Pakistani Air Force planes and were believed to have the tacit support of the military leadership.[16] Differently, India has been the recipient of great international trust in a way that arguably weakens the non-proliferation regime. The Nuclear Suppliers Group (NSG) – a group of forty-nine supplier countries who collaborate to ensure that nuclear trade does not contribute to proliferation – implicitly endorsed a 2005 agreement between India and the United States to approve trade in uranium and nuclear technology, by exempting India from NSG rules 'barring co-operation with states outside the NPT that do not accept nuclear safeguards on all their nuclear facilities'.[17] Eight Indian nuclear power plants were kept outside IAEA safeguards, potentially enabling the production of up to 400 weapons worth of weapons-grade plutonium annually. As well as creating a damaging double standard in the regime, the US–India deal was viewed by Pakistan as a direct threat to its national security and spurred the introduction of Theatre Nuclear Weapons (TNWs) into its conventional land battle doctrine.[18] Israel – which maintains a posture of nuclear 'opacity', neither confirming nor denying its possession of nuclear weapons – is not believed to have transferred technology abroad and has in fact bombed nuclear facilities in Iraq and Syria.

As this book was being completed, it was clear that the NPT bargain was under considerable stress. Non-nuclear weapon states were becoming increasingly frustrated at what they perceived to be a reversal of progress on disarmament, at the same time as many of them were reluctant to agree to increased controls on proliferation and the nuclear fuel cycle – measures that will be important if the world is ever to abolish nuclear weapons. The 2015 NPT Review Conference ended in failure and acrimony and states had decided to step outside the procedural framework of the NPT and develop a new multi-lateral venue for dialogue about a treaty that could ban nuclear weapons entirely. These developments are taken up in Chapter 6, along with some of the more innovative strategic thinking that has set out an achievable path towards the complete elimination of nuclear weapons in this century.

The nuclear Anthropocene

In August 2016 a scientific working group of the International Commission on Stratigraphy presented its recommendation that a new geological epoch – the 'Anthropocene' – be declared to have superseded the Holocene, because humanity's collective impact on planet Earth has been so profound that it will be found in the geological record. They assessed that the epoch began in approximately 1950 and that one of its key signatures, along with plastic pollution, increased atmospheric carbon dioxide, nitrogen in soils and chicken bones, was the global distribution of radioactive elements from nuclear weapons testing.[19] In many ways this prominence of the nuclear age in the scientists' recommendation is apt; indeed one can argue it does not go far enough. Atmospheric nuclear testing has left concentrations of the radioactive isotope strontium-90 in the bones of almost every human being and, by the 1980s, Earth system scientists were publishing papers arguing that not only would a major nuclear war destroy much of Europe, the Soviet Union and the United States, it would cause such intense global cooling that it would create a new Ice Age.

If there is a submerged and recurring theme running throughout this book, it is just this kind of enormity and the implications that it holds for human societies and our systems of national and global governance. The physical enormity of being able to unleash forces that hitherto had operated only in the centre of stars; the planetary enormity of creating weapon systems that in their most extreme hours of interaction could destroy much of the biosphere and change the climate; the moral enormity of machines that alone could destroy a city and together could imperil the very life of the planet. The political, moral and ethical questions are profound. Who is allowed to decide to use and manage these powers? Small groups of politicians, bureaucrats, scientists and military officers, or a democratic polity of global citizens and the communities these powers will most affect? Who decides what kind of technologies will be made from them and for what purposes? Who can manage the contradictions which arise when these purposes clash, or give rise to profound harms in the course of utilizing the mineral for good? Can a global system based on the sovereign rights and powers of states be trusted to manage the dangers and potentials of uranium, or will a new cosmopolitan global governance architecture need to be created? In short, are we, as a political species, truly capable of managing the ethical, environmental, strategic and political complexities unleashed by the modern exploitation of the uranium atom?

CHAPTER TWO

The Brief History of a Resource

The geopolitics of uranium begins with the discovery of the neutron, the ultimate subversive. The neutron is a tiny, neutrally charged particle that, like its partners the proton and electron, lies at the inner heart of all matter. When neutrons are slowed down and slipped into the nucleus of a large unstable atom like uranium, the nucleus is irreversibly destabilized, decaying into lighter elements and in the process generating astonishing amounts of energy.[1] The amount of energy produced is expressed in the famous equation distilled by Albert Einstein in 1905 – $E=mc^2$ – energy equals mass times the speed of light squared. In the three decades between the discovery of the atomic nucleus by Ernest Rutherford and the full understanding of the awesome power of nuclear fission (by Lise Meitner, Otto Frisch, Otto Hahn and Fritz Strassman), quantum physics moved from an obscure and abstract discipline to one that lay at the core of major powers' war plans and national security policies. Rutherford proposed the existence of the atomic nucleus in 1910 and 'split' the atom in 1919; in 1933 Enrico Fermi confirmed the hunch of Leo Szilard that a 'chain reaction' – wherein neutrons expelled from fissioning atoms generate further fissions – could be achieved by bombarding uranium-235 with slowed neutrons; and in December 1938, when Meitner and Frisch had their insight about the fission of uranium, Europe was lurching into war.

In 1938, we were on the threshold of a new world. The next seven years saw a possibility hinted at in scientific papers and anxious conversations transformed into massive national enterprises in the UK, USA and Soviet Union, incorporating hundreds of thousands of workers and billions of dollars of expenditure. It was at this time that work developed in small private labs was moved into highly classified government facilities controlled by the military and intelligence services and open publication of sensitive research findings was suspended. Whereas, until the late 1930s, open scientific publishing and communications spread atomic knowledge freely (in 1939 there were more than 100 papers published on nuclear fission), after 1940 results were kept secret and countries like the Soviet Union resorted to spying. A key paper by French scientists, published in *Nature* in April 1939, revealed that three to four neutrons were emitted per fissioning atom of uranium-235. However Leo Szilard had sought to delay the publication of the paper (after successfully convincing Fermi to delay a similar paper slated for publication in the *Physical Review*) but was rebuffed by the French team of Frederic Joliot-Curie based at the College De France. Joliot was a former assistant of Marie Curie and married to her daughter.[2]

The French confirmation that a chain reaction was possible – which had been earlier revealed in a February 1939 issue of *Nature* by Lise Meitner and Otto Frisch – triggered governmental action in four major powers. A professor at Imperial College, G. P. Thompson, wrote to the British government to alert them to the possibility of using fission to make unprecedentedly powerful bombs and to the need to secure the uranium held by Union Minière in Belgium. In Germany, the Army Ordnance Department set up a project to study nuclear fission and the Ministry of War took over the Kaiser Wilhelm Institute for Physics in Berlin. It also banned the sale of uranium from the mines it now controlled in Czechoslovakia. In France, Joliot-Curie told the government of uranium's possibilities and a military intelligence officer was sent to Norway to retrieve the 185 kg of heavy water owned by the Norsk Hydro Company. After the Nazi invasion of France two of Joliot-Curie's co-authors escaped to England with the water, while he remained behind.[3]

The new scientific secrecy – and a German error – was crucial in slowing the German programme. Fermi did not publish his discovery that pure graphite was an efficient neutron moderator for nuclear reactors; having mistakenly ruled this approach out, the Germans focused on heavy water, which was far scarcer.[4] In the United States, Leo Szilard began efforts to alert the federal government. After unsuccessfully meeting with an admiral at the Department of the Navy, he and Edward Teller (later to invent the hydrogen bomb) obtained Albert Einstein's signature on a letter to President Roosevelt which was presented to him in October 1939.[5] Yet it was not until the very end of 1941 that the Manhattan Project was formally established under the leadership of General Leslie Groves and a civilian physicist, Robert Oppenheimer. A key trigger was the July 1941 report of the UK MAUD Committee which laid out concrete scientific and industrial guidance for the production of a bomb. One of Groves' first decisions was to purchase 1,250 tons of Belgian uranium, mined in the Congo, then sitting in the port at Staten Island. Less than three years later atomic bombs of two different kinds would have been made, tested and used against cities.

The early years of research saw enduring themes emerge around the moral and geopolitical consequences of atomic weapons. Some scientists worried about the ethics of devoting scientific efforts to such a destructive weapon, but reassured themselves that it was necessary to deter Germany from using a potential bomb of its own. Thus the idea of 'deterrence' found its way into our strategic language. Some wondered if the enormity of the weapon would lead to the abolition of war itself, possibly through the formation of a world government. Thus began efforts to 'internationalize' control over the technology and global reserves of uranium. Others, like Niels Bohr, worried about the radically destabilizing consequences of a technology that could not be incorporated within the existing concepts of war that saw armed forces as violent means to a political end. Churchill told him bluntly that the bomb would bring no change in the fundamental principles of warfare.[6]

A key scientific detail explains why uranium became so coveted and why so much of it was required to build atomic weapons. Uranium occurs naturally in the form of two isotopes: U-238 (which has 92 protons and 146 neutrons) and U-235 (which has 92 protons and 143 neutrons). U-238 is the most abundant in nature, with only 0.72 per cent being in the form of U-235 which is scattered in trace quantities throughout uranium ores. U-238 is not fissile, being unable to host a self-sustaining chain reaction, but is a highly unstable element, radiating alpha particles and decaying (via Thorium-234 and Proactinium-234) into Uranium-234. It can also, by absorbing a slow neutron, beta-decay into the highly fissile Plutonium-239, which was used to create the implosion bomb and is a source of fuel for nuclear reactors. The early atomic scientists quickly realized that they would have to isolate large amounts of U-235 to create fissile cores for bombs and that this presented a major technical challenge.[7] U-235 is only present in natural uranium at around 0.72 per cent, making its concentration a complex, time-consuming and technologically challenging process.[8] For example, it required a vast industrial enterprise and six months to produce the 64 kg of enriched U-235 for the Hiroshima bomb.[9] This difficulty is something we should be thankful for; it is the enabling secret at the heart of the non-proliferation regime.

The race for uranium

Uranium gets its name from a Berlin chemist, Martin Klaproth, who in 1789 obtained a sample of a mysterious waste product from an old silver mine in Bohemia, St Joachimsthal. After heating it in solution and then adding wax and oil, he isolated a heavy grey residue that had the properties of a metal. He decided it was a new element and named it after the newest planet in the Solar System and the ancient Greek god of the sky, Uranus.[10] The unwitting classical roots of the element's name would have a dark and prophetic poetry to them, testifying to its terrible powers of creation and destruction. As described in Hesiod's *Theogony*, Uranus (sky) was created by Gaia (mother earth) and mated with her to produce the twelve Titans, three Cyclopes and three Hecatonchires – the latter whom he hated and hid inside the earth. Angered, Gaia then gave their Titan child Cronus a sickle, which, in a brutal act of revenge, he used to cut off Uranus' sexual organs. The sperm that fell in the ocean created the goddess Aphrodite, while the blood created the Giants, Meliai and Erinyes (the Roman Furies). The Erinyes – two of whom are named Alecto (unceasing) and Tsiphone (vengeful destruction) – were sworn to punish those who gave false oaths, committed evil acts, or indulged in hubris.[11] As the frequent reference to another Greek myth by writers on the nuclear age attests – the story of Prometheus – hubris was a constant, ironic presence during the Cold War. Meanwhile the second US intercontinental ballistic missile (ICBM) design was a volatile, liquid-fuelled, multi-megaton behemoth named the 'Titan'. The first? 'Atlas'.

Until scientists began experimenting with radioactivity in the late nineteenth century, uranium was a kind of hidden secret, present and poorly known, its stunning powers obscured by the uses humans had for other things. It has been found as a colouring agent in stained glass used in Roman mosaics and was used as a yellow colouring for body paint and art by American indigenous tribes. In the fifteenth century the Bohemian peasants at St Joachimsthal discarded the black substance as a waste rock they called *pechblende* (pitchblende, or 'bad luck mineral', because its presence meant the coveted seams of silver mined to smelt coin had run out and new shafts must be dug). Yet locals began to succumb to a fatal lung disease that began with a hacking cough and spitting blood.[12] It would be another four centuries before anyone understood why.

The initial commercial uses of uranium were to create yellow glass with a green fluorescence and colored glazes for ceramics. Uranyl nitrate was used in early photography to give a sepia tint to prints and films.[13] Even when research into radioactivity developed in the early twentieth century and its medical applications as a way of treating cancer developed, uranium was primarily valued as uranite, the ore body from which element 88 – radium – could be extracted. The laboratory run by Marie Curie was devoted to working with radium, a much rarer element she had discovered in 1898. The mine at Shinkolobwe in the Belgian Congo, where 'the purest bubble of uranium ore ever found on the earth' was discovered in 1915, was initially mined for radium. Most of the uranium ore was discarded as tailings. Things would change in 1942, when a US Army Colonel working for the Manhattan Project arrived to buy the tailings and have them shipped to the United States. The mine went on to become a major source of uranium for the early atomic bombs and the US nuclear arsenal over the next two decades. Groves contracted with Union Minière to supply four hundred tons per month of uranium oxide from its Congolese mine, which was reopened with the assistance of US Army engineers. In a strange coincidence, 1235 pounds of powdered uranium oxide, left over from Germany's abortive bomb research, came to the Manhattan project from a U-Boat which surrendered to the US Navy, after being en route to Japan as Germany fell to the Allies. As the war in Europe ended, Groves ordered the capture of German atomic scientists and the remaining German uranium stocks, which were soon to come under Soviet control. When US forces found themselves unable to secure a processing plant at Oranienburg, which was in the Russian zone just north of Berlin, Groves ordered that it be bombed.[14]

Other sources for the Manhattan Project included the El Dorado mine in Canada, on the Eastern shore of Great Bear Lake near the town of Port Radium. Cold War supplies of uranium for US programmes were sourced from numerous mines on the Colorado plateau, many of them on the vast Navajo reservation across Arizona, New Mexico and Utah. Groves believed uranium was only present in a few locations and that the USA could control all sources of the mineral and have a long atomic monopoly. The USA established the Combined Development Trust with Britain for precisely this purpose and signed agreements in 1945 with the Netherlands, Brazil and Belgium (and obtained an informal assurance from Sweden) to prevent the sale or transfer of uranium to the USSR. Groves boasted that the trust countries controlled 97 per cent of global uranium output and 65 per cent of the thorium production.[15] His estimate of global reserves, however, was soon to be proven wrong. Groves' error about the ubiquity of uranium is further underlined by considering how later nuclear powers sourced their supply. Both China and South Africa were able to mine uranium locally; it was gaining access to reactor technology, U-235 and weapons designs that was more challenging. The same is true for Pakistan and India. Pakistan has been able to source uranium locally, from the mine at Lakki, while India sourced its uranium from the mine at Jaduguda, which began production in 1967. A very large new deposit was found in 2011 at Tummalapalle in Andhra Pradesh.[16]

When the Soviet nuclear programme officially began in April 1943, supplies of uranium were scarce. A 'Commission on the Uranium Problem' was established in 1940, but geologists had no idea what domestic uranium reserves existed. An immediate priority was to build an experimental reactor, much like Fermi's at the University of Chicago, to produce plutonium. Graphite was chosen as the moderator, a substance used to slow down neutrons for facilitating fission, because the construction of a plant to make heavy water would take until after the war. However a graphite reactor required more uranium. Initial parts for a cyclotron were retrieved from a Leningrad still under siege by the German army. Igor Kurchatov, the scientific director of the new Soviet programme, required 50–100 tonnes of uranium for the reactor but had access to less than two tonnes. It was also difficult to obtain graphite of the required purity, which did not become available until after the war. Ironically, some early supplies – 400 kg of uranium oxide and uranium nitrate, along with 1,100 grams of heavy water – were acquired from the United States through the Lend-Lease programme. Soviet scientists also obtained between 240 and 340 tons of uranium oxide from Germany and Czechoslovakia after Germany fell to the Red Army.[17]

The key would be domestic reserves. A search commission established in September 1945 uncovered significant reserves and by 1948 mines were opened in the Ukraine, Estonia, Leningrad, the Caucasus and Siberia. Soon, the USSR would be producing large amounts of uranium from mines in Germany, Poland, Bulgaria, Czechoslovakia and Xinjiang. The material basis for a nuclear complex that would eventually build 37,000 nuclear warheads and feed thirty nuclear power plants was being made. The Stalinist context was also relevant: prison labour from the gulag was used to mine uranium throughout the USSR and to build new towns and the weapons laboratory at Arzamas-16. Workers in Eastern Europe were also forcibly drafted to work mines in appalling conditions. There were no safety standards and many workers contracted cancer.[18]

Manhattan

At a meeting in Princeton in 1939 between key American-based physicists, Niels Bohr told Eugene Wigner, Edward Teller and John Wheeler that, while a bomb was theoretically possible, it would be impossible to separate enough U-235 'unless you turn the United States into one huge factory'.[19] Allowing for hyperbole, it was exactly this that the Manhattan Project was designed to do. It would involve the expenditure of $1.8 billion and draw on the labour of 130,000 people. Sites were established across the USA and Canada: reactors, production and separation plants, laboratories, testing ranges, heavy water plants and mines. Fermi established a research reactor in squash courts under the University of Chicago's football stadium, in the middle of an urban area. The major reactor and production sites were the Hanford Engineering Works, on the Columbia river in Southeastern Washington and Oak Ridge in eastern Tennessee. Eighty per cent of the cost was to produce the fissile cores of the bombs, with the uranium enrichment plants at Oak Ridge costing $1.1 billion alone.[20] The electromagnet at the Oak Ridge plant weighed tons and required miles of copper wire, a metal then in shortage. Instead, $300 million in silver from the US Treasury was used – 13,500 tons – and returned after the war.

The scale of the enterprise in part reflected a desire for speed, as it did in the Soviet Union. Efforts were made to produce two different fissile metals – U-235 *and* plutonium – and to use both gaseous and thermal diffusion methods in combination. In turn, the weapons laboratory established under Robert

Oppenheimer's leadership at Los Alamos developed two different bomb designs: one, using U-235 to create the explosive chain reaction, the other, plutonium. In each case, the ease of producing the material was in inverse relationship to the difficulty of designing a bomb around it. Scientists quickly determined that the simple 'gun' design of the uranium bomb – in which a hollow cylinder of highly enriched uranium (HEU) is explosively shot into a second cylinder of U-235 to create a super-critical mass – was likely to work and would not need testing. Yet, given how long it would take to produce the required amount of HEU, only one could be made by the end of 1945. This became 'Little Boy', the bomb used against Hiroshima on 6 August 1945. In contrast, the design for the plutonium weapon – which required the spherically uniform explosive compression, or 'implosion', of a sub-critical mass of plutonium – was extraordinarily challenging. It took up almost all of the scientific effort at Los Alamos, involving thousands of staff and a budget of $74 million.[21] The plutonium weapon became 'Fat Man', the bomb used against Nagasaki on 9 August 1945. The nicknames for the bombs – including the first abandoned gun design, 'Thin Man' – came from Dashiel Hammett's detective fiction and *Film Noir*. Fat Man and Thin Man were characters from *The Maltese Falcon*.

Profound political, ethical and strategic questions would emerge as the research drew to fruition and Berlin fell in May 1945. What was the purpose of the weapon, especially if Germany had been subdued? Should it be used in the war? If so, should it be held in reserve as a threat, or used in a devastating attack? And, given that the science of making atomic bombs was now proven and likely to be replicated elsewhere, what impact would the new technology have on the making of war and the conduct of international relations? What choices would shape the ways in which this astonishingly active matter – uranium – would affect numerous post-war societies?

In a way that would become typical of national security policy-making – and remains one of its most problematic features – decision-making power about the bomb's military uses would remain closeted and secretive, restricted to the president and a few senior military officers. In the midst of a terrible war, humanity was not able to debate, or even know about, a weapon that would alter the very condition of being human. Yet as the war with Germany ended and the Trinity test of the plutonium weapon approached, the Los Alamos scientists became increasingly concerned about how the bomb would be used and its post-war implications. The Polish physicist Joseph Rotblat – who had earlier worked with James Chadwick and Otto Frisch in Manchester – left Los Alamos in December 1944, as it became clear Germany was nearing defeat and their bomb programme had stalled in its early stages. In his mind, both the strategic and moral case for the bomb had collapsed. Earlier that year – in what Rotblat coyly termed 'a disagreeable shock' – Groves told him and Chadwick at dinner that 'you realize of course that the whole purpose of this project is to subdue the Russians'.[22]

Around the time Rotblat left, Robert Wilson organized a meeting of scientists at Los Alamos to discuss 'the impact of the Gadget on civilization'. A key issue, according to one participant, was 'whether the country is doing the right thing in using this weapon on real live human beings'. Oppenheimer discouraged Wilson from holding the meeting, but nonetheless turned up. At least three other meetings were held over the next few months, including a colloquium in March 1945 attended by forty scientists, to discuss 'the atomic bomb in world politics'.[23] There many gave vent to deep moral disquiet, along with profound and prescient thinking about the impact of the technology on future war and international order. However, Rotblat was the only one to leave the programme. According to his biographers, Oppenheimer's intervention at the March meeting was influential:

Wilson recalled that Oppenheimer dominated the discussion ... The war, he argued, should not end without the world knowing about this primordial new weapon. The worst outcome would be if the gadget remained a military secret. If that happened, then the next war would almost certainly be fought with atomic weapons. They had to forge ahead, he explained, to the point where the gadget could be tested. He pointed out that the new United Nations was scheduled to hold its inaugural meeting in April 1945 – and that it was important that the delegates begin their deliberations on the postwar world with the knowledge that mankind had invented these weapons of mass destruction.[24]

In contrast to his principled and incisive writings after the war, Oppenheimer's arguments here were draped in bad faith.[25] First, as Victor Weisskopf recounts, Oppenheimer had initially discouraged the meetings with arguments that 'as scientists they had no right to a louder voice on the gadget's fate than any other citizen' and that 'this is not our task, and this is politics, and we should not do this'. Yet no citizens knew of the bomb. It was referred to in code – in Washington as S1, at Los Alamos as 'the gadget' – and Los Alamos scientists had gotten drunk in various bars in town with the aim of spreading rumours they were working on electric rockets. Second, momentum was inexorably building to move directly from a test to its use against Japan, momentum of which Oppenheimer was well aware. An alternative purpose as a deterrent, whether virtual or actual, was in the mind of no military officer or strategic policy-maker at the time. As Gerard DeGroot writes, 'the Bomb was a weapon in search of a role'.[26]

In May 1945, Secretary of War Stimson formed an 'Interim Committee' to consider immediate post-war policy dilemmas about the weapon. Its work also discussed the question of its use in Japan. The Committee included a four-member 'scientific advisory panel' drawn from the Los Alamos scientists – Oppenheimer, Ernest Lawrence, Fermi and Arthur Compton – and while the broader community of scientists may have hoped the group would represent their moral concerns, they were given short shrift. Lawrence raised a suggestion of Robert Wilson's – that the power of the weapon be demonstrated to Japan, perhaps by inviting them to witness a test – in a key meeting of the Interim Committee on 31 May.[27] On this day, the scientists gave the committee a grim briefing on the bomb's likely explosive yield (up to 20,000 tons of TNT) and effects on human life and debated the proposal for a demonstration. However the consensus, supported by Oppenheimer, was that given the risks of the weapon failing either to explode or impress the Japanese, this option should not be tried. Later that afternoon the committee agreed 'that we should not give the Japanese any warning; that we could not concentrate on a civilian area; but that we should seek to have as profound a psychological impression on as many inhabitants as possible'.[28] Stimson had also established a 'Target Committee', of which Oppenheimer was a member and Groves the dominant voice. Groves wanted military targets big enough to test and demonstrate the awesome power of the weapon, which meant cities. As McGeorge Bundy explains, 'while every city proposed had quite traditional military objectives inside it – like an army headquarters, or harbor installations, or factories producing military supplies – the true object of attack was the city itself. The planners placed the aiming point, in every case, at the centre of the built up area.'[29] In short, when the weapon was tested on 15 July 1945, it was in full knowledge of what would come next.

At the University of Chicago Leo Szilard – who, we should recall, began the momentum towards an American bomb by preparing the 1939 Einstein letter to Roosevelt – was deeply concerned both about the prospect of the weapon's use against Japan and its potential to create grave insecurity in the

post-war world order. In the weeks leading up to the Interim
Committee decision, Szilard and Einstein again wrote to
Roosevelt warning that the use of the bomb would precipitate
an arms race with the USSR. After Roosevelt died without
reading the letter, they wrote to Oppenheimer with the same
warning and obtained a meeting with Truman's Secretary of
State designate, James F. Byrnes. He batted their concerns
away by claiming that Groves had told him there was no
uranium in Russia and the use of the bomb against Japan may
persuade the Soviets to withdraw their forces from Eastern
Europe. A group of Chicago scientists led by Szilard then
produced a 12-page report to Stimson, known as the Franck
report, opposing the Bomb's use on Japan and recommend-
ing a demonstration of the weapon before representatives of
the United Nations, at a desert or barren island. It warned,
chillingly, that 'if no efficient international agreement is
achieved, the race for nuclear armaments will be on in ear-
nest not later than the morning after our first demonstration
of the existence of nuclear weapons'. Its case was both moral
and strategic. It expressed grave concern about the impact of
a dispersed nuclear attack on US cities and industry and highlighted that nuclear weapons represented 'an indiscriminate
method of wholesale destruction of civilian life': 'the military advantages and the saving of American lives achieved
by the sudden use of atomic bombs against Japan may be
outweighed by the ensuing loss of confidence and by a wave
of horror and repulsion sweeping over the rest of the world'.
The Army quickly classified the report, but its contents were
briefed to Oppenheimer and others at Los Alamos. Szilard
then circulated a petition which gathered 155 signatures from
Manhattan Project scientists. Reflecting an argument in the
Franck report, the petition argued that Japan should not be
attacked without the terms of surrender being made public
and Japan having rejected them.[30]

It was all to no avail. The military and the Truman administration, not the scientists, were in control of the deployment of the weapon and had long been set on its use. In parallel with the testing of the plutonium weapon and further weapons construction as Los Alamos, the Air Force was tasked with selecting an aircraft – the new B-29 Superfortress – and establishing a base at Tinian from which to launch the attacks. Pilots practised new manoeuvres to deliver the weapon and avoid its blast. The target committee had chosen Hiroshima, Kokura, Kyoto, Niigata and Nagasaki – although Stimson later excluded Kyoto because of its cultural significance – targets that were to be bombed in succession to destroy Japanese morale.[31] One of the more critical Los Alamos physicists, Freeman Dyson, later told a documentary that the use of the atomic bomb in Japan 'was almost inevitable . . . simply because all the bureaucratic apparatus existed by that time to do it . . . the president would have had to have been a man of iron will to put a stop to it.'[32] Truman had no such will; he held the view that 'I regarded the bomb as a military weapon and never had any doubt that it should be used'.[33]

The notion that the bomb was a military weapon was only sensible against the background of the appalling development of 'strategic' – that is, saturation – bombing during the Second World War. Japan and Germany had begun the practice of indiscriminate bombing of cities and civilians with attacks on Warsaw, London and Chongqing. The Royal Air Force soon began similar tactics in raids on Germany. The US Air Force initially insisted on daylight raids aimed at military targets, but joined the RAF in a brutal eight-day devastation of Hamburg in July 1943, which created a massive firestorm and killed over 42,000. A similar firestorm, lit with the deliberate use of incendiaries, occurred during the three-day bombing of Dresden in February 1945, killing 25,000. Under the command of General Curtis LeMay – later head of the Strategic Air

Command – incendiary bombing was brought into the Pacific theatre and deployed against Japanese cities throughout 1945. LeMay flew his bomber formations at 5000 feet at night, replaced much of their defences with incendiaries and aimed to make cities burn.[34] The campaign began with a devastating attack on Tokyo on 9 March that killed more than 80,000 and extended to Nagoya, Osaka, Kobe, Kagoshima, Toyama and some sixty other cities.

The clear outlawing of strategic bombing as a war crime would wait until the adoption of Additional Protocol I to the Geneva Convention in 1977, which condemned as indiscriminate 'an attack by bombardment by any methods or means which treats as a single military objective a number of clearly separated and distinct military objectives located in a city, town, village or other area'.[35] However the 1922 Washington Conference established an international commission of jurists, who drafted a convention termed 'the Hague Rules on Air Warfare'. It included provisions that aerial bombardment must be directed exclusively against targets of a military character and that 'aerial bombardment for the purpose of terrorizing the civilian population, of destroying or damaging private property not of a military character, or of injuring non-combatants, is prohibited'. Not a single state signed the convention and it was never discussed at a conference.[36] Despite the resulting legal ambiguity, there was a keen appreciation that saturation bombing was morally wrong. Former US Secretary of Defense Robert S. McNamara, who as an air-force colonel worked as a systems analyst for LeMay and produced a study that contributed to the decision to resort to firebombing, later commented: 'LeMay said that if we had lost the war we would have been prosecuted as war criminals. I think he was right. He, and I would say, I, were behaving as war criminals'.[37]

Hiroshima and Nagasaki

It was as if the very air had caught fire. 'Little Boy' exploded over Hiroshima at 8:16 a.m. on 6 August. As the chain reaction cascaded through eighty generations of Einstein's diabolical equation, a bell-shaped fireball exploded in a flash of light that reached a million degrees celsius, as hot as the surface of the sun. Neutron, x-rays and gamma rays saturated the city as the bomb detonated at 1,900 feet directly over the Shima hospital, killing everyone inside. The flash blinded everyone within a kilometre; the heat reduced their bodies to char. Temperatures on the ground reached 4,000 degrees, enough to melt iron and roof tiles and turn sand to glass. The blast and shock waves destroyed all brick structures within a three-kilometre circle and all wooden structures a further two kilometres beyond that. Wind speeds reached 440 km per second; the blast pressure, thirty-two tonnes per square metre. Outside the inner circle of devastation (the 'hypocentre'), the wooden structures left standing caught fire; these fires then quickly merged into a massive firestorm that blocked out the sun, burned for hours and killed those trapped in the rubble of the city. At one school, where teachers lay over the children in an attempt to protect them from the fire, witnesses afterwards found small, blackened human skeletons clinging to adult ones in the playground.[38]

Thirty per cent of the city's people – 70,000 to 80,000 – were killed in the blast and firestorm, but as many survived, at least for a few hours and days, to find themselves in a strange kind of hell, maimed by a weapon they had not previously known of and did not understand. Survivors found themselves covered in burns and gravely dehydrated, shards of glass in their skin, hair smouldering, their skin peeling from their fingers and bodies or fused to their clothes. Others lost their eardrums and eyes in the blast, or tried to hold their organs in with their hands. The wounded thronged roads out of the city centre in their thousands, past rivers and streets choked with dead, so many it was impossible to see the water. The explosive residue, dirt and smoke billowed into what some survivors called a vast 'jellyfish cloud' that hung over the city, first emitting a 'fierce light' of ever-changing colours, then eventually turning dirt-brown. Moisture then condensed and fell on the city as an oily, sooty, radioactive rain. Paul Ham writes that after sundown, as the 'stem of the mushroom cloud lingered', the survivors on the hills surrounding the city 'looked down on the first night of the nuclear age; the bowl of Hiroshima held the city's embers like the crater of an active volcano'.[39]

Three days later, on 9 August, a second B-29 flew from Tinian loaded with the plutonium bomb designed by the Los Alamos scientists, 'Fat Man'. Its initial target was Kokura, which was shrouded in smoke from the bombing of Yawata the night before and had anti-aircraft defences and after three aborted runs they diverted to Nagasaki, which was home to Japan's largest Christian community and whose only significant military facility, a Mitsubishi torpedo factory, lay primarily underground. It exploded with nearly twice the explosive yield of 'Little Boy' – 22 kilotons – and wreaked similar devastation. 1,400 of 1,500 schoolchildren and most of the teachers at one elementary school in the hypocentre were killed, and another junior high was obliterated. Survivors reported chasing dragonflies in the playground one minute and seeing their friends burned and blackened the next, suddenly turned into 'hideous monsters . . . making croaking noises'.[40]

In Hiroshima alone, cremation teams burned 33,000 corpses. Total estimates of the casualties just on the day of the bombs, are 115,000 at Hiroshima – 78,000 dead and 35,000 wounded, out of a city population of 320,000 – and at Nagasaki, 69,000 – 39,000 dead and 30,000 wounded, out of a city population of 260,000. Total mortality from the attacks is reckoned at

160,000 in Hiroshima (dwarfing the already horrific total from the Tokyo firebombing) and 80,000 in Nagasaki. Particularly sinister was the massive subsequent mortality from radiation sickness, including the fetal mortality: all pregnant survivors within a kilometre of the blast miscarried, at 2–3 km only a third gave birth to healthy babies, and two months after the attack the incidence of miscarriage, abortion and premature birth was running at 27 per cent.[41]

Both the bombing and the subsequent actions of MacArthur's occupation authority represented profound violations of international humanitarian law and basic humanitarian values. We know that the bombings would have been a gross violation of 1977's Additional Protocol I to the Geneva Conventions, but even in 1945 they violated what weak injunctions existed (in the 1907 Hague Convention) against area bombing because the pilots reported that both Hiroshima and Nagasaki were almost entirely undefended. The bombings also damaged the fundamental infrastructure of civilian life and survival, with the hypocentre of the Nagasaki bomb in fact being directly over a medical and educational district. The Nagasaki University hospital, less than a kilometre from ground zero, contained 75 per cent of the city's beds. Desperate aid stations were set out where the burns of the wounded were treated with cooking oil. Relief teams struggled through conventional bombardment to reach Hiroshima, but lacked medicines, dressings, clothing, food and beds. People died in their thousands in makeshift shelters, first from dehydration, burns and shock, later from a mysterious new illness: radiation sickness. Ham writes that 'in an instant, Nagasaki's medical system ceased to exist'. While local doctors puzzled to understand the symptoms of radiation sickness, the Americans had a good understanding of it which they refused to share either with the American press or Japanese medical teams. The conclusions of several Allied investigations, which were included in the report of the

Joint Commission for the Investigation of the Atomic Bomb in Japan, were not shared with Japanese doctors, whose own preliminary research was in fact confiscated by occupation forces. One Japanese professor condemned MacArthur's censorship, saying that 'to forbid publication of medical matters is unforgivable from a humanitarian standpoint'.[42]

The strategic rationale for the attacks has long been an issue of great controversy. Debate has centred on whether the attacks were necessary to achieve Japan's surrender and forestall an allied land invasion costly in military life and on whether two bombs were necessary. The attack on Nagasaki proceeded according to a military timetable and the decision was taken without President Truman's direct involvement. It occurred three days after Hiroshima and a day after the Soviets declared war and began to devastate Japanese forces in Manchuria. Four hours before Nagaski was bombed, Japan's emperor and civilian government agreed to accept the allied surrender terms set out at Potsdam, save for a clause retaining the Japanese emperor as an institution. However meetings of the Supreme Council for the Direction of the War and the full cabinet would wait until later in the day and the decision could not be communicated to the allies until they had met. After meeting all day, at 2 a.m. they finally sought direction from Hirohito, who decreed acceptance of surrender. Nagasaki had been a burning hell for fourteen hours. The message was sent at 7 am and accepted by Truman and his cabinet that day.[43]

Groves thought of the atomic bombings as a 'one-two punch' that should be administered to induce a swift surrender. Yet, however terrible, the bombings weighed little in the Tokyo cabinet's deliberations; rather, it was the imminent destruction of the Japanese divisions in Manchuria that was most alarming. When Truman ordered an end to the atomic bombing Groves was frustrated, as he was now presiding over a 'production line' that would have six plutonium weapons ready by October and another in November. The conventional air war did not cease until 14 August and six further cities were added to the atomic target list.[44]

The attack on Nagasaki was clearly appalling and unnecessary; a larger question was whether either of the attacks were necessary to achieve Allied war aims. The Allies' terms were unconditional surrender, but it had been known in Washington since July that the Japanese foreign ministry was seeking to convey, via the Soviets, that surrender would be much more likely if the terms were altered to preserve the emperor. Figures as senior as General George Marshall, US Army Chief of Staff, sought to influence the Allies to soften the terms. While there were plans to begin a ground invasion of Honshu in November, it was thought that both Japan's military weakness – its navy was effectively defeated and its land forces in Southeast Asia and the Pacific stranded at the end of broken supply lines – and the Soviet attack in Manchuria, would be enough to induce a surrender. Evidence also exists to show that both Stimson and Secretary of State Byrnes thought of the bombing as a demonstration of strength that would preclude a Soviet role in the occupation of Japan and make them more pliable in Europe.[45] Indeed Groves thought Soviet entry into the war was a strong rationale for the timing of the Nagasaki attack.[46] Historians divide on how influential the Soviet factor was, but agree that a dark machinery was in operation that ensured Japanese cities would be successively obliterated with nuclear weapons until the President put a stop to it.[47]

Anticipations of the nuclear future

Within seven years, US and Soviet scientists would have tested a new nuclear weapons design – the 'fusion' or 'thermonuclear' weapon – that dwarfed the explosive power of the bombs used in Japan many hundredfold: weapons that were able to create zones of total destruction 30–50 km across and spread fires and radioactive fallout over thousands of kilometres. These facts, and the extraordinary growth in the numbers of the weapons and their combined potential for devastation, highlighted a prescient concern of the dissident Los Alamos scientists: the impact the weapons would have on the conduct of war and the management of international relations. This had been at the forefront of the concerns of Bohr, Szilard, Wilson and others, and was even discussed in meetings of Stimson's Interim Committee. In 1944 Bohr had drafted a private memorandum, which he shared with Oppenheimer and others at Los Alamos. Its key points were that atomic bombs were 'weapon[s] of unparalleled power which will completely change all future conditions of warfare' and that 'unless some agreement about the control of the use of the new active materials can be obtained in due time, any temporary advantage, however great, may be outweighed by a perpetual menace to human security'.[48]

The Franck *Report to the Secretary of War* of June 1945 – which primarily addressed itself to 'the post-war organization of nucleonics' – also advocated a system of cooperative international control, based on a prescient argument that no state would be able to develop effective defences against the weapons or retain a strategic monopoly on their possession. Even without knowledge of the destructive potential of the H-bomb, it warned that atomic bombs three times as powerful as 'Fat Man' were within reach and that a large number of them dispersed across major cities and industries would have a devastating effect on the United States. They also warned of a problem that would plague Cold War nuclear strategy: the temptations of a first strike. The report concluded profoundly that:

In the past, science has often been able to provide new methods of protection against new weapons of aggression it made possible, but it cannot promise such efficient protection against the destructive use of nuclear power. This protection can come only from the political organization of the world . . . in the absence of an international authority which would make all resort to force in international conflicts impossible, nations could still be diverted from a path which must lead to total mutual destruction, by a specific international agreement barring a nuclear armaments race.[49]

Humanity has not yet been able to conclude such an agreement. The NPT was able to limit the proliferation of weapons between states but not within them and the prospect of realizing the current proposal for such a treaty – a Nuclear Weapons Convention – is far off. However even after Bohr had been rebuffed by Churchill when he tried to expound his fears of an atomic arms race in May 1944, in the war's immediate aftermath American policy-makers made serious if abortive efforts to respond to such concerns. An important document, known as the Acheson–Lilienthal Report, drew on both the ideas of the Los Alamos scientists and a communiqué from Truman, British Prime Minister Clement Attlee and Canadian Prime Minister Mackenzie King. It boldly advocated an international authority that would have a monopoly on all 'dangerous' nuclear activities (including uranium and thorium mines, enrichment and weapons research) but was vague on disarmament.[50] Many are now arguing it is time to revisit such ideas, which will be addressed again in Chapter 6.[51]

In the late 1940s the USA made a proposal to the new United Nations Atomic Energy Commission (known as the 'Baruch Plan') which included the Acheson–Lilienthal proposals, an intrusive international inspections regime and a view that great power veto should not be able to prevent international enforcement. However, the USA would only contemplate relinquishing its growing stock of atomic bombs once an international authority had been established, while the Soviets countered with a proposal for an international convention to prohibit the development, storage, or use of atomic weapons and require their elimination. The discussions dragged on while both countries were testing and researching new weapons – including the H-bomb – and were moribund by 1948.[52] Instead, a terrifying new future opened in which hopes of restraint would rest on a single strategic idea, expressed by Bernard Brodie in 1946: 'thus far the chief purpose of the military establishment has been to win wars. From now on its chief purpose must be to avert them.'[53]

CHAPTER THREE

Weapons and Security

In 1980 the superpowers possessed more than 54,000 nuclear warheads between them. Many of the weapons were on high alert, ready to be launched within a few minutes of warning that an attack was under way, and they possessed a combined explosive power that could destroy life on earth many times over. They were divided between a 'triad' of strategic (long-range) nuclear forces that included intercontinental ballistic missiles (many of which had multiple 'MIRVed' warheads with distinct targets), long-range bombers and submarines. US–Soviet relations were extremely tense and moving into their most dangerous years since the Cuban missile crisis in 1962. At the same time, debates in the USA about nuclear strategy, war-fighting and targeting doctrine were taking an extraordinary and alarming turn. Think-tank strategists with political and defence connections were railing against the unofficial doctrine of 'mutual assured destruction' established in the late 1960s by Secretary of Defense Robert S. McNamara, which saw nuclear forces as primarily a deterrent against attack by the other side. Nuclear war plans envisaged large attacks against Soviet nuclear forces designed to limit the devastation to one's own country and had been estimated to result in the deaths of hundreds of millions if they were ever carried out.

These conservative strategists, who worried about moral restraint resulting in a kind of 'self-deterrence', wanted to be able to wage nuclear war *politically* if it became necessary: to

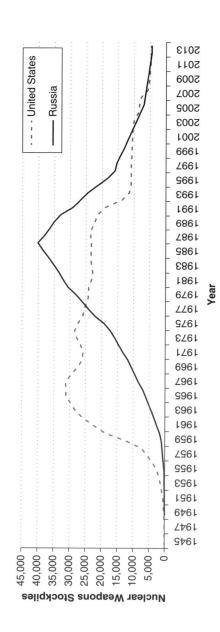

Graph 3.1: Nuclear Weapons Stockpiles 1945–2013: USA and Russia

Source: Hans M. Kristensen and Robert S. Norris, Global Nuclear Weapons Inventories, 1945–2013, *Bulletin of the Atomic Scientists,* 69 (5). 2013, Table 2, 78.

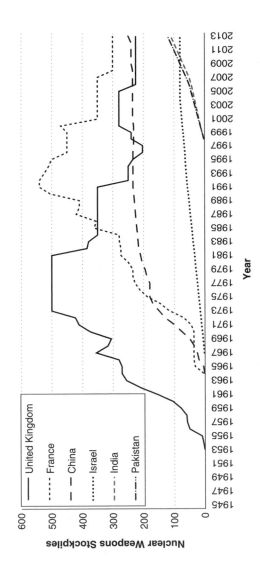

Graph 3.2: Nuclear Weapons Stockpiles 1945–2013: UK, France, China, Israel, India, Pakistan

Source: Hans M. Kristensen and Robert S. Norris, Global Nuclear Weapons Inventories, 1945–2013, *Bulletin of the Atomic Scientists,* 69 (5), 2013, Table 2, 78.

launch more limited attacks and bargain with the weapons that remained. This was the view of Richard Nixon's Secretary of Defense James Schlesinger and influenced revisions to the US nuclear war plan (the SIOP).[1] However, even these 'intra-war bargaining' strategies were too timid for the Hudson Institute scholars Keith Payne and Colin Gray, who published articles in 1980 arguing for the USA to develop a 'war-winning strategy' that would combine missile defences with devastating strikes that would target and destroy 'Soviet political authority and [bring about] the emergence of a postwar world order compatible with American values'.[2] After the nineteenth-century Prussian strategist Carl Von Clausewitz, they wanted to use (nuclear) war as 'a form of politics by other means'; as a military means to a political end. Despite the fact that national missile defence – which their plan relied on to restrict US casualties to some twenty million – was still an entirely fanciful technology, within three years key elements of their plan were incorporated into the SIOP and came close to having to be put into action.

In the month of September 1983, a Korean Airlines flight was shot down by Soviet fighters after straying into Soviet airspace, killing 263 passengers and outraging Americans, and a Soviet early warning station mistook sunlight reflecting from clouds over the United States for five Minuteman missiles en route to the USSR. Then in November, two weeks after the US invasion of Grenada, which removed a Soviet-allied government, NATO conducted high-level military exercises – code-named Autumn Forge and Able Archer – to test their command and control during the transition from conventional to a nuclear war in Europe. The exercises included a drill for NATO defence ministers on the stages involved in initiating nuclear war and the movement of NATO forces from alert levels DEFCON 4 through 1. The KGB concluded that US nuclear forces had been placed on alert and 'might even have begun the countdown to war'. Already alarmed by Reagan's announcement of a Strategic Defense Initiative (SDI) missile defence and the deployment of Pershing II missiles to Europe, the Soviets feared that the exercise was cover for a first strike (a stratagem to be found in their own war plans). Months earlier, they had initiated a major intelligence exercise to watch for signs of pre-emptive attack. Until the Able Archer exercise finished three weeks later, Soviet aircraft in Eastern Europe remained poised to counterattack. These events were only two of at least thirteen documented cases of the near use of nuclear weapons in war and numerous other accidents with nuclear weapons.[3]

Weapons and security: key questions

This vignette, based on just a few months in one year during the Cold War, exemplifies the great complexities and dangers of nuclear weapons when applied to national and international security. It demonstrates powerfully the theme identified in Chapter 1: that the volatile agency of the uranium atom frustrated the more hubristic attempts to weaponize it and that there were many ways to exploit its potential, which was always likely to transform and challenge our social and international systems and generate appalling ethical dilemmas. The Cold War is when many of these choices were made, locking the world into a prison of its own making. It is especially striking that the Able Archer crisis was almost entirely created by the combination of nuclear doctrine and weapon systems: a toxic mix of MIRVed weapons, launch-on-warning postures, war–fighting nuclear doctrine and missile defence that is now widely understood to be destabilizing. In both September and October 1983 anxieties were so high and warning times were so short, that nuclear war based on misperception was a serious possibility. This chapter considers the relationship

between nuclear weapons and security by asking a fundamental question: whose security were the weapons meant to
serve and could they ever do so? If it was national security,
how could that be reconciled with the extraordinary level of
threat that American and Soviet citizens would be exposed to?
If it was global security, what are we to make of the fact that
the national security strategies of the superpowers threatened
the globe with catastrophe? Was it particular nuclear policies
and strategies that made us more or less insecure, or were
the weapons themselves, as Niels Bohr warned, a 'perpetual
menace to human security'?[4]

The chapter also traces the evolution of key strategic nuclear
doctrines in major countries during the Cold War and since,
to assess their impact on global security. Two themes emerge.
Firstly, even though mutual assured destruction has been a
kind of bedrock situation, classical deterrence has not actually
been tried. Nuclear weapons have not been used solely to deter
other nuclear weapons but rather have been intended for a
range of missions including conventional war, which has only
added to their destabilizing impact. Secondly, nuclear doctrine
has regularly sought to make the weapons usable as a tool of
coercion and of warfare. When such nuclear strategies are
examined closely, they founder on their own contradictions –
they have never been able to envisage nuclear weapons having
utility without the risk of widespread catastrophe.[5] Such thinking still remains influential among civilian strategists, military
officers and political leaders responsible for nuclear weapons
and is a major obstacle to disarmament. A related problem
is the way that many political leaders see nuclear weapons as
conferring prestige and power on their states. The fact that
the permanent membership of the United Nations Security
Council are all nuclear weapons states is an unfortunate, if
telling, coincidence. All of those states possess a *veto* on the
majority vote of the Council's membership and use it with-

out compunction. This means that, even as the possession of nuclear weapons is seen as fundamentally illegitimate under the NPT, possession plays a very different role in the structure of global security governance. There, nuclear weapons are an element of great power dominance.

At the same time, the confidence in deterrence is on the wane, with more and more former leaders, ministers and nuclear commanders calling for safer nuclear postures and total disarmament. Notable interventions in recent years have come from the so-called 'Gang of Four' – former US Secretaries of State Henry Kissinger and George Shultz, former Secretary of Defence William Perry, and Chairman of the Senate Arms Services Committee Sam Nunn – and the NGO *Global Zero*, which published a report endorsed by global military leaders urging the de-alerting of nuclear weapons and their rapid elimination.[6] Fears of nuclear accident and terrorism are driving this loss of faith in nuclear strategy and a new movement concerned with exposing the humanitarian implications of nuclear war has questioned the value of nuclear weapons for national security and exposed the danger they pose to global security. Three major international conferences held in Mexico, Norway and Austria in 2013 and 2014 shifted the discourse away from the abstract language of deterrence to consider the devastating impact on human societies, ecosystems and the biosphere if nuclear weapons were actually used.[7] Pope Francis, the leader of 1.2 billion Catholics, told the Vienna conference that 'the humanitarian consequences of nuclear weapons are predictable and planetary' and that 'nuclear deterrence and the threat of mutually assured destruction cannot be the basis for an ethics of fraternity and peaceful coexistence among states'.[8]

At the UN General Assembly in 2013, 124 states presented a joint statement expressing grave concern about the 'deep implications [of nuclear war] for human survival; for our environment; for socio-economic development; for our economies; and for the health of future generations' and insisting that the 'only way to guarantee that nuclear weapons will never be used again is through their total elimination'. The same statement was presented to the 2015 NPT Review Conference on behalf of 159 states. By the end of that conference, 107 states had endorsed a document drafted by Austria after the Vienna conference, known as the 'Humanitarian Pledge', in which states commit to 'efforts to stigmatize, prohibit and eliminate nuclear weapons in light of their unacceptable humanitarian consequences and associated risks'.[9]

Early Cold War dilemmas

Realist international relations scholars like Kenneth Waltz argue that the introduction of nuclear weapons into world affairs helped to keep the peace during the Cold War, 'if peace is defined as the absence of general war among the major states of the world'. This is, in his view, because deterrence in the form of mutual assured destruction worked by raising the costs of war and inducing caution in the actions and policies of statesmen. Indeed, he argued late in his life that nuclear weapons were 'the best peace-keeping weapons the world has ever known . . . we should count our nuclear blessings'.[10] The record does not support Waltz's confidence. He overestimated the stability of the Cold War deterrence system and the levels of nuclear safety around weapons and during geopolitical crises. On many occasions, the world came far closer to nuclear war than he allows and, if we grant that the devastating prospect of nuclear war did prevent major conventional conflict between great powers, it came at the price of enormous planetary risk. Nor did nuclear weapons prevent the superpowers supporting numerous brutal so-called 'limited' and proxy wars – such as those in Korea, Afghanistan, Vietnam, Cambodia, Indonesia,

El Salvador, Nicaragua and Ethiopia – which caused the deaths of millions. There was no 'long peace' for them.

This is one particularly sanguine interpretation of the relationship between nuclear weapons and international security. Yet at the outset of the Cold War, how nuclear weapons would affect the security of states and peoples was less clear. It would, in large part, depend on the choices of the nuclear powers themselves. In the USA, the early Cold War brought two somewhat contradictory perspectives. The military and some atomic scientists sought to push on with nuclear weapons and missile research, to build up the US arsenal and create new delivery capabilities that could be used both to defend the United States and pressure the USSR. This was the short-lived period of the so-called 'atomic monopoly'. Other scientists and strategists held fears that they may not be able to solve the puzzle of national security in a nuclear armed world. As Bernard Brodie asked, would society be given 'the opportunity it desperately needs to adjust its politics to its physics'?[11]

Atomic monopoly and war in Korea
The atomic bomb proved to be a blunt weapon in diplomacy. The USA had sought to intimidate the Soviets with the bomb in the 1945 negotiations about Romania and Bulgaria, but were ignored by foreign Minister Molotov, and Stalin called off his planned invasion of the major Japanese Island of Hokkaido, not because of the terrible demonstration at Hiroshima, but because Hokkaido was not a part of the mutually recognized 'sphere of interests' agreed between the great powers at Yalta.[12] Soviet officials had visited Hiroshima and Nagasaki and concluded that the bombs had a limited strategic effect; Soviet military doctrine held that victory in war would be decided on land and by the combination of 'permanent factors', not 'by one king of a weapon alone'. However Soviet weapons research was well under way under the

command of the brutal NKVD chief Beria and Stalin was determined to end the US monopoly as soon as possible. The USSR exploded a fission bomb in 1949 and a fusion bomb in August 1953 – less than a year after the first American hydrogen bomb test in November 1952 – and began work on ICBMs in 1947, well ahead of the United States.[13] Meanwhile the US atomic monopoly was in fact accompanied by strategic anxiety: military planning in the late 1940s envisaged a first strike either in retaliation for Soviet aggression or to prevent it developing an atomic capability that could threaten the USA; that is, a preventive nuclear war. The strategic logic appeared to be that, whereas in the past offence was seen as the 'best means of defence, in atomic warfare it will be the only general means of defence'. Truman rejected preventive war, declaring that it would be 'the weapon of dictators'.[14]

The relative weakness of US and Western European land forces vis-à-vis the Soviets created a strategic dilemma – to which an answer seemed to be the atomic bomb. In the first Berlin crisis of 1948, when the Soviet restrictions on allied rail access were relieved by an airlift, the Joint Chiefs of Staff asked if atomic bombs may be available – but they were not. A small stockpile of plutonium weapons existed but all assembly teams were in the Marshall Islands preparing for the *Sandstone* tests of fission weapons with a much larger explosive yield (up to 47 Kt) than those used against Japan.[15] This stimulated efforts to create plans to transfer weapons to the military and create a standing capability. Prior to the first Soviet atomic tests the US military developed war plans for Europe (HALFMOON) with an annex that envisaged full-scale atomic attack on the USSR with 50 bombs with the aim of causing the 'paralysis of at least 50% of Soviet industry'. Truman rejected the atomic annex and demanded a solely conventional war plan, but the thinking presaged the 'massive retaliation' policy that the Eisenhower administration adopted in 1954.[16]

The war in Korea was another test of atomic utility. Nine atomic weapons and aircraft to deliver them were sent to Guam in August 1950 for possible use against North Korean, Soviet and Chinese targets, but they were never launched. Nor were the smaller yield 'tactical' (battlefield) nuclear weapons used, even though they were successfully tested in 1953. UN force commander General Douglas MacArthur urged that they be used against North Korean supply lines and bases in Manchuria and the dangers of general war rose in April 1951 when the USSR moved 200 bombers to bases in northern China and threatened to use them if the USA attacked China. Both Truman and the Joint Chiefs of Staff proved reluctant to use the weapon in a 'limited' war for three reasons: moral qualms about using the weapon against an underdeveloped country; strategic doubts that the weapons would materially affect the outcome of the war; and concerns that, had it become evident that the weapons were militarily ineffective, their psychological power as a deterrent to Soviet forces in Europe would have been undermined. However, such moral doubts about the use of the atomic bomb did not extend to the weapons that had been used so devastatingly against Japan: firebombing. Whereas jellied gasoline was used against Japan, a new weapon, napalm – a mixture of acids and phosphorus that can burn inside wounds for days – was introduced in Korea. The use of incendiary bombs against industrial and military targets still destroyed, in the estimate of a key air-force general, '40–90' per cent of North Korea's towns and cities. These attacks, and the destruction of six major dams which destroyed the rice crop, made a major contribution to the death of over two million civilians.[17]

The H-bomb

The decision to build the hydrogen (or thermonuclear fusion) bomb dramatically affected the world's future security. In the

USSR research on the hydrogen bomb closely followed that on the fission bomb and there was effectively no separate decision to go ahead with the programme.[18] In the United States, however, the decision to build 'the Super', as it was termed, was a momentous one that was contentiously debated. It became caught up in Cold War paranoia and McCarthyite hysteria, while ushering in a vastly more insecure age. The fission weapons already developed and used were alarming enough; the fusion weapons would have major humanitarian and strategic impacts because of their dramatically greater explosive power per unit of radioactive material. This meant enormously greater material devastation and loss of life from their use and the ability to build many more weapons using the same amount of uranium and plutonium. This directly fuelled the arms race between the two superpowers and imperiled the life of the planet.

There are two basic designs of fusion weapons, both of which also utilize nuclear fission as a large component of their explosive yield. The 'boosted fission' weapon achieves yields up to 500 Kt and as low as 20 t of TNT (as a tactical or battlefield weapon). It is the plutonium implosion bomb redesigned so that the spherical shell of plutonium is hollow and includes a gaseous mixture of two isotopes of hydrogen (deuterium and tritium). The initial fission explosion produces such high temperatures that it causes the atoms of deuterium and tritium to fuse, emitting enormous amounts of neutrons that increase the intensity of the ongoing fission reactions. The USA tested two boosted fission weapons at Enewetak atoll in 1951 with yields of 225 Kt and 45 Kt; the tests demonstrated the potential of thermonuclear fusion and proved a weapon which would become the first stage of the (two-stage) H-bomb. The first Soviet thermonuclear nuclear test of August 1953 was a different kind of boosted fission weapon (the 'layer cake') that used a much larger amount of hydrogen and achieved a yield of 400 Kt. Its mushroom cloud rose twelve kilometres into the atmosphere and the stem was six kilometres across. The earth was turned to glass for five kilometres surrounding ground zero and its destructive aftermath was described by one observer as inspiring 'flesh creeping terror'.[19]

The true 'Super' would exceed this terror manyfold. It was a two-stage weapon that used a boosted fission weapon as a source of the x-rays and heat that would create the 'temperature[s], pressure and density greater than that found at the centre of the sun' which are required for large-scale nuclear fusion. Both devices are contained within a casing of uranium-238; the fission device contains layers (working inwards) of high explosive, beryllium, plutonium-239 and deuterium-tritium gas; and the fusion device has layers of U-238/U-235, lithium-deuteride and a central 'sparkplug' of U-235, which intensifies the already extraordinary heat and compression in the explosion. The whole assembly could be made less than 2 metres long – small enough to fit in the nose cone of a missile, a MIRV warhead or a slim air-delivered bomb.[20] This design could create weapons of theoretically unlimited destructive power: the first US H-bomb test, 'Mike', yielded 10.4 Mt (10,400,000 tons of TNT), while another, 'Bravo', had an unexpected yield of 15 Mt. In 1961 the USSR tested a three-stage hydrogen bomb (which combined one fission and two thermonuclear devices) that yielded 50–54 Mt and created a mushroom cloud 64 km high that reached into the mesosphere. Had the weapon been encased in a U-238 rather than lead tamper it could have exploded with 100 Mt of energy. Even though its 8 metre long assembly could be flown in a specially modified aircraft, weapons of this size were never deployed.[21]

The USA deployed 9 Mt warheads on the Titan II missile (and 9 Mt bombs in B-52 bombers) during the 1960s and 1970s, although the successor programme, Minuteman, used

1.2 Mt warheads that could be launched within minutes of an alert (and until the New START treaty had three MIRVed 300 Kt warheads). During the 1950s the USA deployed 10-Mt bombs (the Mk-17 and Mk-24), while the largest deployed US weapon was the Mk-41 bomb, a terrifying 25 Mt three-stage weapon. Used against a densely populated city like Moscow, a single 9 Mt weapon would have vaporized everything in a 17 km² circle, spread lethal radiation across a 35 km² circle, damaged or destroyed buildings within 650 km² and spread heat intense enough to start fires and cause third degree burns across a circle 700 km wide and 3700 km² in area. It would have killed over five million people and injured four million more. A 300 Kt weapon (such as the W-87 warhead on the currently deployed Minuteman III missile) would spread devastating heat across 200 km², kill 650,000 people and injure 2.3 million more.[22] Cold War operational plans also provided for multiple weapons to be targeted at major cities.

By 1953, when the first Soviet thermonuclear tests took place, the USA had 1169 atomic [fission] bombs compared to the USSR's 120. The 'Mike' test had taken place only a few months before. The Soviet leadership perceived themselves to be well behind in an arms race and saw the H-bomb as a means to end what one Central Committee member called a 'threatened second [thermonuclear] monopoly for the Americans'. Whereas the design of the Soviet fission bomb owed much to its spies within the Manhattan Project, it developed the designs for the boosted fission weapon and the two-stage fusion bomb independently. Soviet anxiety about the limitations of its Air Force also led to an early decision to develop the intercontinental ballistic missile (ICBM), which then took more than a decade to develop and deploy.[23] In the USA, the Pentagon and the Truman administration were keen to develop the 'Super', but problems with the research allowed time for internal debate among scientists. (The flaws in Edward Teller's initial design – conceived in 1946 – could only be revealed by laborious calculations, many of which were carried out by the first (room-sized) computers, ENIAC and MANIAC. Françoise Ulam and Teller only published a paper outlining a new (successful) two-stage bomb in March 1951, while the 'Mike' test that proved the concept took place in November 1952. This delay did not prevent Senator Joseph McCarthy claiming in April 1954 that 'communists in government delayed "our research on the hydrogen bomb" by 18 months' – which set the stage for an Atomic Energy Commission hearing that stripped Oppenheimer of his security clearance and severed him from bomb research.[24]

As Chair of the General Advisory Committee of the AEC (GAC), Oppenheimer did harbour strategic and moral doubts about the H-bomb, but they were in fact more muted than those of others. An October 1949 meeting of the GAC canvassed a range of views, including the JCS, and drafted a report that unanimously opposed development of the H-bomb. The unlimited explosive potential of the bomb was the overwhelming concern. The report said that 'it is not a weapon which can be used exclusively for the destruction of material installations of military or semi-military purposes. Its use therefore carries much further than the atomic bomb itself the policy of exterminating civilian populations.' It also foresaw 'possible global effects of the radioactivity' and recommended countering a Soviet H-bomb with the current US stock of fission bombs. The Manhattan Project physicists Enrico Fermi (who created the first chain reaction) and I. I. Rabi also wrote a blistering annex that advocated an effort at arms control – the President, they argued, should 'invite the nations of the world to join us in a solemn pledge' not to build thermonuclear weapons – and condemned the H-bomb in moral and humanistic terms:

> Necessarily such a weapon goes far beyond any military objective and enters the range of very great natural catastrophes.

> By its very nature it cannot be confined to a military objective but becomes a weapon which in practical effect is almost one of genocide . . . the use of such a weapon cannot be justified on any ethical ground which gives a human being a certain individuality and dignity even if he happens to be resident in an enemy country . . . the fact that no limits exist to the destructiveness of this weapon makes its very existence and the knowledge of its construction a danger to humanity as a whole. It is necessarily an evil thing considered in any light.[25]

Truman, however, had made up his mind and was more influenced by the Joint Chiefs of Staff who argued that:

> the United States would be in an intolerable position if a possible enemy has the bomb and the United States did not . . . public renunciation by the United States of super bomb development might be interpreted as the first step in unilateral renunciation of the use of all atomic weapons, a course which would inevitably be followed by major international realignments . . . the security of the entire Western hemisphere would be jeopardized.[26]

According to his press secretary, Truman felt that there 'actually was no decision to make on the H bomb . . . we had to do it . . . though no one wants to use it. But . . . we have got to have it if only for bargaining purposes with the Russians.' Richard Rhodes suggests that strategic considerations were of lesser weight: 'the decision was urgent politically: the military and a vocal, organized segment of Congress would fight him if he decided not to build the Super'.[27]

McGeorge Bundy argues that two other, linked, options were worth considering: the notion of a 'thermonuclear test ban agreement' proposed by Fermi and Rabi, with no verification machinery other than the ability to detect a nuclear test through 'national-technical means' (atmospheric readings and seismographic observation), possibly coupled with an agreement that research could continue but that no bombs should be tested or built. These ideas were never seriously explored within the White House or the State Department.[28] A historian of the Soviet bomb project, David Holloway, also considered this possibility and concluded that Stalin and NKVD chief Beria were too distrustful of the United States to have reciprocated, even if a serious diplomatic offer had been made. It is impossible to speculate about such a counterfactual, but later years would show that arms control agreements with the Soviets were possible and that they would be driven by mutual fears of strategic instability and the consequences of nuclear war. It was undoubtedly a lost opportunity to ban, by mutual agreement, a particularly destructive and destabilizing weapon system – similar to Henry Kissinger's later regret that he had not pursued an opportunity to ban the MIRVed missile during arms-control talks in the 1960s and 70s.[29]

After Stalin's death, Soviet leaders such as Malenkov began to talk openly of the potential for world war to lead to 'the end of world civilization' and of the need for 'further weakening of international tension [and] a stable and durable peace'. Krushchev spoke of how, after receiving his first full briefing on the nuclear situation, 'I could not sleep for several days. Then I became convinced that we could never possibly use these weapons, and when I realized that I was able to sleep again. But all the same we must be prepared. Our understanding is not sufficient answer to the arrogance of the imperialists.' After seeing the thermonuclear tests Igor Kurchatov (Oppenheimer's equivalent as scientific director of the Soviet programme) told a colleague that it 'was such a terrible, monstrous sight. That weapon must never be allowed to be used!' H-bomb inventor Andrei Sakharov worried that 'this newly released force could slip out of control and lead to unimaginable disasters', while a group of senior officials and atomic scientists (which included Kurchatov) wrote an incisive article about the likely consequences of nuclear war. They argued that, given current rates of production, there would soon be enough atomic explosives 'to create on the whole globe conditions impossible for life . . . the explosion of about 100 large hydrogen bombs would lead to the same result . . . one cannot but acknowledge that over the human race there hangs the threat of an end to all life on earth'.[30] Truman himself felt grave moral doubts, which he expressed in his last State of the Union speech of 1953:

> . . . no advance we make is unattainable by others [and] no advantage in this race can be more than temporary. The war of the future would be one in which man could extinguish millions of lives at one blow, demolish the great cities of the world, wipe out the cultural achievements of the past, and destroy the very structure of a civilization that has been slowly and painfully built up through hundreds of generations. Such a war is not a possible policy for rational men.[31]

There is a terrible irony about this part of the Cold War: a clear awareness, on both sides, of the terrible nature of the world that they were making and an absolute inability to refrain from making it.

Crises, strategy and arms control

What was being made was a world in which all kinds of nuclear weapons – from multi-megaton hydrogen bombs to smaller 'tactical' (battlefield) nuclear weapons with yields between 0.5 and 15Kt – were being built and deployed in ever greater numbers. This production in many ways preceded the existence of rational strategies for their deployment or use and raised a profound strategic puzzle. (Later, strategies would also drive production, with increased target lists and 'selective options' – that is, nuclear war-fighting doctrines – driving up warhead numbers.) What would their effect or role be in a crisis? Would they be useful or dangerous? Could they be used on a battlefield? Could (or should) they only be used to deter other nuclear weapons or could they be used to deter conventional war? And what if deterrence failed? Could a nuclear war be fought and won? Could it be controlled – and survived?

The US nuclear production complex received major funding increases in 1950 and 1952. The Hanford and Oak Ridge plants doubled in size and two new gaseous-diffusion plants to separate U-235 were created; these drew so much electricity that by 1957 the AEC consumed 6.7 per cent of the total US power supply. By 1955 the AEC's capital investment was nearly $9 billion, more than General Motors, US Steel, Alcoa, DuPont and Goodyear combined. US weapons numbers increased from 369 in 1950, 4600 in 1956, to over 27,000 in 1962, the year of the Cuban missile crisis. By that year the USSR had some 3346 bombs and warheads. Just as alarming – given the crises to come – was the explosive yield of the weapons deployed during the 1950s and 1960s: the total megatonnage of the US arsenal increased from 339 Mt in 1954 to 20,491 Mt in 1960 – and was still a staggering 12,825 Mt (much of it in 3421 strategic weapons) in 1962.[32] When we consider that the Soviets armed their ICBMs with very large warheads and that a single 9 Mt weapon had the potential to destroy a 3700 km^2 area, it is possible to get a sense of the extraordinary latent devastation in both arsenals.

Massive retaliation
Even as the notion of deterrence (of nuclear attack) had by now emerged as the major background rationale for the accumulation of nuclear arsenals on both sides and Truman officials had come to doubt the utility of nuclear weapons for any other purpose, the Eisenhower administration sought to make nuclear weapons useful on the battlefield and as a major deterrent to conventional war in Europe. Concerned about NATO's conventional weakness, they introduced tactical nuclear

weapons into Western Europe and developed a doctrine of 'massive retaliation' for any Soviet attack – conventional or nuclear – out of the Eastern Bloc into the West. This was set out in NSC–162/2, *Basic National Security Policy*, as well as in speeches by the Secretary of State John Foster Dulles. The major focus of the policy was Europe, as the deputy commander of NATO explained in 1954: '[we] are basing all our planning on using atomic and thermonuclear weapons in our defence. With us it is no longer, "they may possibly be used". It is very definitely: "They will be used, if we are attacked".' However, in a policy known as 'brinkmanship', Dulles sought to inject a note of doubt about what kind of response the USA would make in a range of other contingencies involving the USSR and China. He believed that subtle nuclear threats had induced China and North Korea to sue for peace in 1953 and broke the diplomatic deadlock that ended the Korean war. The use of tactical nuclear weapons was also considered in support of French forces at Dien Bien Phu – and would have been used, had the Joint Chiefs of Staff not been convinced that they would have to follow with a large deployment of American forces.[33] The USSR took the challenge of the atomic battlefield seriously, holding an exercise in the southern Urals in 1954 with 44,000 troops. A medium-yield nuclear weapon was detonated 6 km from the two sides' trenches and the defending side attacked with 700 high-explosive bombs and long-range artillery. Troops were sent into the blast and radiation zone and officers 'were impressed by the power of the bomb, but they did not regard it as something so terrible so to make war unwageable'. Lessons learned on the nuclear battlefield were incorporated into the 1955 Soviet Field Regulations.[34]

The massive retaliation strategy and its blurring of conventional and nuclear war had two profound problems. First, in a truly diabolical moral equation, the Administration and NATO commanders were proposing to take tens (if not hundreds) of

millions of Russian civilian lives and destroy the basis of civi-
lized life to forestall the loss of tens or hundreds of thousands
of NATO military personnel. Second, was the inbuilt likelihood of strategic failure. NATO commanders did not consider
the potential for battlefield use of nuclear weapons to esca-
late to general war and they were overly sanguine about the
growing Soviet capability to retaliate and devastate the cities
of Europe and the United States. Between 1952–9 its arsenal
increased from 50 to 1,048 (including 283 strategic weapons)
and the first ICBM (the R7/SS-6) was first deployed in 1958.[35]

Just as concerning were discussions in the Strategic Air
Command (SAC) and US Air Force circles about the need
for a pre-emptive (or even preventive) attack on the USSR
during the 1950s before it had an effective retaliatory capacity. Soviet generals and strategists conducted similar debates.
Eisenhower ruled out preventive war, but the resulting
pre-emptive 'blunting mission' given to SAC was an early
version of the 'launch-on-warning' posture adopted once the
Minuteman solid-fuelled ICBM was deployed. SAC commander Robert LeMay also sent multiple reconnaissance
aircraft over Vladivostok at noon one year and bombers at
other times deep into the USSR; historians speculate he may
have been trying to provoke nuclear war, out of his belief
that 'there was a time in the 1950s when we could have won
a war against Russia. It would have cost us essentially the
accident rate of the flying time, because their defences were
pretty weak.' Ironically this thinking coincided with a growing joint awareness of the mutual devastation that a nuclear
war would create. At Geneva in 1955 the first meeting since
Potsdam between the superpowers took place and Eisenhower
and Marshall Zhukov speculated that an exchange of 600
hydrogen bombs, given the prevailing East–West winds,
would create 'fallout [that] might destroy entire nations and
possibly the whole northern hemisphere'. Zhukov is said

to have stated that he was 'unqualifiedly for total abolition of weapons of this character'. The meeting achieved little beyond overflights in Eastern Europe as a security-building measure – a system of mutual early warning – but the Soviet proposal for a nuclear test ban, which the USA rejected, was to be prescient.[36]

By the 1960s, the USSR was still well behind in weapons and delivery systems but an effective stalemate – a 'balance of terror' – had been reached. Robert Oppenheimer still has the most eloquent account of such a situation, from an essay of 1953:

> . . . during this period the atomic clock ticks faster and faster. We may anticipate a state of affairs in which two Great Powers will each be in a position to put an end to the civiliza- tion and life of the other, though not without risking its own. We may be likened to two scorpions in a bottle, each capable of killing the other, but only at the risk of his own life. This prospect does not tend to make for serenity.[37]

The Cuban crisis
There was no serenity to be had. As the Kennedy administra- tion took office in early 1961 it quickly found itself in a series of Cold War crises in which nuclear weapons and threats took an ever larger role. A number of destabilizing policies and events culminated in the Cuban missile crisis: Soviet efforts to use nuclear threats to dramatically change the *status quo* in Berlin essentially failed with the construction of the Berlin wall in August 1960; the same year, an American U2 spy plane was shot down over Russia and the superpower summit in Paris was cancelled; in April 1961 the botched CIA- sponsored invasion of Cuba was repelled at the Bay of Pigs; and in October 1961, Deputy Secretary of Defense Roswell Gilpatric gave a speech that underlined, both to allies and the USSR, the overwhelming nuclear strategic superiority then

held by the USA: 'this nation has a nuclear retaliatory force of such lethal power that any enemy move that brought it into play would be an act of self-destruction on his part . . . we have a second strike capability which is at least as extensive as what the Soviets can deliver by striking first'.[38]

McGeorge Bundy argues that this public statement (and the actual capability it referred to) helped to deter any kind of Soviet military move on West Berlin – although the Americans had also been building up conventional defences. It also directly contributed to the Cuban missile crisis. The Soviets – yet to deploy ICBMs in any significant number and with many thousands fewer bombs – had significant anxieties about their relative nuclear weakness, the security of the Castro regime and their political standing in Latin America.[39] This led to Krushchev's dangerous decision during 1962 to secretly deploy a threatening mix of forces to Cuba: 40,000 troops; parts for 42 IL-28 bombers; anti-aircraft missile batteries; 36–42 medium range ballistic missiles (MRBMs) with a range of 1100 nautical miles, each carrying a one megaton warhead and capable of reaching Washington DC in less than five minutes; and 80 tactical cruise missiles (with a yield of 2 Kt each) and twelve Luna short-range tactical missiles (12 Kt) for use against US invading forces. U2 spy flights over Cuba on 14 October revealed the MRBM sites and triggered the crisis; over the next thirteen days, as they debated possible military responses – including massive airstrikes and a full invasion of the island – US officials were apparently unaware of the presence of tactical nuclear weapons and underestimated the number of Soviet troops.[40]

Kennedy demanded that the missiles be removed from Cuba and instituted a naval quarantine that prevented a further 24 intermediate range ballistic missiles (IRBMs) with a range of 2200 nautical miles from reaching Cuba. He also ordered US military forces to DEFCON3 on 22 October and then

DEFCON2 on 24 October, the highest state of readiness for nuclear war short of actual conflict. This alert state lasted for days and involved the dispersal of nuclear bombers to civilian airports and the placing of 1,479 bombers, 182 ICBMs and 112 Polaris SLBMs on high alert. Between 66 and 72 B-52 sorties (each carrying between two and five multi-megaton bombs) were flown around the edges of the Soviet Union every day. 250,000 troops were readied for an invasion.[41] The stakes were made clear by Kennedy in a televized speech of 22 October, when he declared that the USA would 'regard any nuclear missile launched from Cuba against any nation in the Western Hemisphere as an attack by the Soviet Union on the United States, requiring a full retaliatory response upon the Soviet Union' and that 'we will not prematurely or unnecessarily risk the costs of worldwide nuclear war . . . but neither will we shrink from that risk at any time it must be faced'.[42]

The crisis was eventually resolved by the USSR agreeing to withdraw the missiles under UN supervision in exchange for a US undertaking not to invade Cuba, along with a secret American promise to remove obsolete liquid-fuelled Jupiter missiles from Turkey. Kennedy resisted the advice of his military advisors – McNamara and the Joint Chiefs of Staff – to conduct an immediate campaign of air strikes or launch a ground invasion of Cuba. He and others worried that this could lead to a chain of escalation – such as a Soviet attack on Turkey or Berlin – that could lead to general nuclear war. However, had the Soviets not yielded so quickly, it is very possible that pressure for an attack on Cuba would have become overwhelming. Only thirty years later did McNamara become aware that tactical nuclear weapons were already deployed and that Soviet forces had been instructed to use them in their defence. He commented that 'no one should believe that had American troops been attacked with nuclear weapons the United States would have refrained from a nuclear response.

And where would it have ended? In utter disaster.' In the film *The Fog of War*, McNamara also recounted a 1992 conversation in which Fidel Castro told him that 'we started from the assumption that if there was an invasion of Cuba, nuclear war would erupt. We were certain about that . . . we would be forced to pay the price, that we would disappear.' When Castro then claimed that he and Kennedy would have done the same in his position, McNamara replied: 'Mr President, I hope to God we would not have done it – pull the temple down on our heads? My God!'[43]

Furthermore, despite the admirable safety record of the Strategic Air Command during the month-long alert, there were still serious risks of nuclear accident or inadvertent war: forced to rush into service a new deployment of Minuteman missiles at Malmstrom Air Force Base, ICBM launch control officers 'jerry-rigged an independent launch capability with inadequate safeguards'; a previously scheduled test-flight of an Atlas ICBM was launched from Brandenburg Air Force Base on 26 October without approval from Washington; and one of the routes flown by the B-52s was considered by the 15th Air Force 'as presenting an unnecessary risk of accidental penetration of Soviet territory' – which had been demonstrated in August that year when a navigational error caused a nuclear armed B-52 to veer 470 miles off course towards Soviet Siberia.[44]

The Cuban crisis led to the establishment of a secure communications link between Moscow and Washington – a teletype system dubbed 'the hotline' – and began the first tentative steps towards superpower arms control. The limited test ban treaty was signed in August 1963 and it entered into force in October, during the first anniversary of the Cuban crisis. It prevented nuclear tests in the atmosphere, outer space and underwater, and was motivated by an awareness of the toxic effects of fallout. The treaty was the product of nearly eight years of discussions and negotiations that were frustrated by disputes over verification and desires to link such a treaty to 'a cut-off in the production of fissionable materials for weapons and safeguards against surprise attack' – issues that remain outstanding on the international non-proliferation agenda today. The breakthrough was achieved in the wake of the Cuban crisis and by removing underground tests from the treaty. However a comprehensive test ban treaty (CTBT) still has not come into force, despite 183 states having signed it; earlier, in 1991, the US government blocked a proposal by Mexico, Indonesia, Peru, Sri Lanka, Yugoslavia and Venezuela 'to extend the LTBTs prohibitions to all environments, transforming the LTBT into a comprehensive test ban'.[45] The USA has maintained a moratorium on nuclear testing since 1992 and has signed the CTBT, but the US Senate has blocked ratification. India, Pakistan and North Korea have not signed the treaty, and Egypt, Israel and China still have not ratified.[46]

Scorpions in a bottle

US nuclear strategy continued to evolve during the 1960s, but did not slow the arms race. McNamara first developed a 'counterforce' or 'no cities' doctrine (which could include more limited nuclear options), which met with much criticism and Soviet hostility. There was still a likelihood of extensive damage to cities and the Soviets were suspicious that the USA would seek to develop a war-winning capability that may make a first strike feasible. They were half right: whereas the administration always sought to avoid war, the US Air Force 'had come to associate counterforce with the ability to fight and win a nuclear war'. This effort to stabilize and increase the credibility of deterrence in fact made it unstable, and the technical requirements for counterforce capabilities and targeting further fuelled the arms race. The introduction of MIRVed missiles (carrying multiple warheads that each have their own targets) further raised fears of vulnerability to a first strike and drove a massive increase in warhead numbers during the 1970s in order to maintain deterrence.[47]

McNamara then adopted the doctrine of Mutual Assured Destruction, a darkly evocative language chosen deliberately to emphasize the appalling consequences of a nuclear exchange. The US nuclear war plan (the SIOP) contained a mix of city and counterforce targets, and each side deployed nuclear weapons in a 'triad' of forces (aircraft, missiles and submarines) that would ensure a second-strike capability. The USA also phased out its European IRBMs, which were vulnerable to attack and only useful in a first-strike. This mutual understanding was, with some difficulty, formalized in superpower arms control in the form of the Antiballistic Missile (ABM) treaty of 1972, which prevented the development and deployment of nationwide ABM systems other than two – one to protect the national capital and the other to protect an ICBM site.[48] In 1970 the Treaty on the Non-proliferation of Nuclear Weapons also entered into force. Its Article VI required all of its members to 'pursue negotiations in good faith on effective measures relating to cessation of the nuclear arms race at an early date and to nuclear disarmament, and on a treaty on general and complete disarmament under strict and effective international control'.[49]

Despite the adoption of the NPT and the ABM treaty's prevention of a technological temptation to first strike, the next three decades were ones of lost opportunity. The Cold War intensified in the second half of the 1970s and overall weapons numbers rocketed to extraordinary levels: by 1987 strategic warhead numbers had peaked at 13,173 for the USA (of a total of 23,575) and 11,320 for the USSR (out of a total 38,187 weapons). An American study conducted for the 1977 Presidential Review Memorandum (PRM-10) estimated that minimum fatalities from a major nuclear war would be

140 million in the USA and 113 million in the USSR and that almost three-quarters of both economies would be destroyed.[50]

Later studies into the atmospheric effects of nuclear war showed that these numbers were probably conservative. Studies by climate scientists published in 1983 (using a 5000 Mt nuclear war as a baseline) described a probable phenomenon of 'nuclear winter', in which the soot lifted into the stratosphere would block out sunlight over much of the northern hemisphere and then move into the southern hemisphere. The models predicted the failure of the Asian monsoon, dramatic decreases in rainfall around the world, destruction of the ozone layer that would expose people to dangerous UV radiation, high levels of delayed radioactive fallout, and intense cooling of between 5 and 35 degrees Celsius that implied 'potential massive crop losses both in low-latitude and mid-latitude regions'. These effects were predicted to last between one and three years.[51] More recent studies, which modelled a nuclear war with the greatly reduced US and Russian arsenals of the mid 2000s, as well as a 'regional' conflict which involves the explosion of only 100 weapons, also predict catastrophic nuclear winter with global effects.[52] In 2010 Carl Sagan recalled how 'in the baseline case, land temperatures, except for narrow strips of coastline, dropped to minus 25 Celsius (minus 13 degrees Fahrenheit) and stayed below freezing for months – even for a summer war . . . virtually all crops and farm animals, at least in the Northern Hemisphere, would be destroyed, as would most varieties of uncultivated or domesticated food supplies. Most of the human survivors would starve.' He concluded that 'the cold, the dark and the intense radioactivity, together lasting for months, represent a severe assault on our civilization and our species'[53] It is not hard to imagine the devastation of human food security, the global economic chaos and the violent conflict that such a crisis would provoke.

Adding to the danger, in the 1970s and 1980s conservative strategists aggressively challenged the doctrine of Mutual Assured Destruction at the same time as they promoted the Reagan administration policy of national missile defence. Thus came the American strategic doctrines of the 1970s and 1980s with which I began this chapter – of limited war fighting and 'intra-war bargaining' on the one hand and nuclear war winning on the other. These options were included in the SIOP and official guidance stated that 'should deterrence fail and strategic nuclear war with the USSR occur, the United States must prevail and be able to force the Soviet Union to seek earliest termination of hostilities on terms favourable to the United States'. Reagan's Secretary of Defense, Caspar Weinberger, affirmed this policy.[54] Strategists such as Desmond Ball understood the potential Soviet response to this policy, one that would lead the world so close to nuclear war during the 1983 NATO Able Archer exercise: 'the plans and capabilities for war-fighting and leadership targeting have been taken to dangerous extremes. The US ability to promptly destroy the Soviet leadership must increase the Kremlin's incentives to act massively and decisively at the onset of a strategic nuclear exchange.' The British strategist Michael Howard commented: 'Few of us believe that there would be much left of our highly urbanized, economically tightly integrated and desperately vulnerable societies after even the most controlled and limited strategic nuclear exchange ... such a war might or might not achieve its object; but I doubt whether the survivors on either side would very greatly care.'[55]

Toxic legacies: strategy and testing

The diabolical conjunction of the Cold War and nuclear weapons left two persistent legacies: one, material, relating to the weapons themselves, their toxic components and the environmental and humanitarian legacy of their testing; the other, ideational and strategic, relating to the persistence of the idea that nuclear weapons can be rational means of national defence or warfare and can be retained indefinitely. Together, they prolonged the harms of the nuclear complex and frustrated the efforts of international society to force the nuclear weapon states to disarm.

When the NPT was negotiated in 1968 and 1969, it embodied in international law an assumption that nuclear arsenals were a grave threat to international security and an immoral means of war. The doctrine of mutual assured destruction could be seen as an at least partial acceptance of this view, but it has not been paired with postures that would create strategic stability – such as declarations that nuclear weapons will only be used to deter other nuclear weapons ('sole use'), that they will only be used in retaliation ('no first use'), and that they will not be used to target non-nuclear weapons states ('negative security assurances', or NSAs). Missiles remain on a hair-trigger 'launch on warning' posture, which dangerously reduces the decision time of leaders in crisis and raises the prospect of a pre-emptive attack in a crisis or accidental nuclear war based on false warnings. This has almost happened on at least four occasions: in 1979 and 1980, when false reports of the major Soviet attack came from NORAD, firstly from an exercise tape left in the system and secondly from a faulty computer chip; in 1983, when Soviet early warning satellites mistakenly reported five Minuteman missiles en route to the USSR; and in 1995, when Norway's launch of a scientific rocket on a trajectory that took it close to Russian territory was mistaken for the launch signature of a Trident SLBM. Russia's loss of its space-based surveillance capacity and the fear of cyber-attack raise further concerns.[56]

The US insistence on pursuing research into missile defence – research that was revived by the George W. Bush

Administration, which unilaterally withdrew from the ABM treaty in 2002 – has soured relations with Russia who consider it a threat to strategic stability and exacerbated other conflicts between Russia and the West.[57] In recent years, these tensions have been especially acute over Georgia, Syria, Iran and Ukraine – which led, in the latter case, to the imposition of sanctions on Russia. In response, Russian leaders have issued veiled nuclear threats and the UN Secretary-General has warned of 'a dangerous return to Cold War mentalities'.[58] Other authors warn that NATO's installation of missile defence sites in Eastern Europe has also been used politically to strengthen the authoritarian regime of Vladimir Putin.[59]

The lingering effects of nuclear weapons testing also remain a significant humanitarian legacy. Testing intersects with many other facets of the geopolitics of uranium: the legacy of colonialism, the impact on indigenous peoples, the arms race and proliferation, global environmentalism and the stunning recklessness of scientists and military managers. Over 500 atmospheric tests were conducted by nuclear powers to 1980 and the number rises to over 2000 when underground tests are included. The National Resources Defense Council has estimated that the total yield of all nuclear tests conducted between 1945 and 1980 was 510 Mt, with atmospheric tests accounting for 428 Mt. Atmospheric testing by China and France continued long after the Partial Test Ban Treaty of 1963; the Comprehensive Test Ban Treaty has still not come into force.[60] While a number of nuclear tests were conducted in Nevada and within the borders of the Soviet Union and China, metropolitan nuclear powers chose to test far from their shores and in ways that dispossessed and endangered indigenous communities and destroyed their livelihoods. Testing also lofted radioactive fallout and isotopes high into the stratosphere, creating global health and security risks. The USA tested in the Marshall Islands, which they took by force from Japan in 1944 and administered as a UN trust territory. Britain tested in the Indian Ocean at the Montebello Islands and Christmas Island (which was captured from Japan and then transferred to Australia) and in the South Australian desert on the lands of the Maralinga Tjarutja people of the Pitjantjatjara. The French tested in Algeria, prior to its independence, and then at Mururoa atoll in French Polynesia.

At Maralinga, seven major explosions were conducted with yields between 1 and 27 Kt, spreading plumes of radiation across to the east coast of Australia, along with hundreds of 'minor' tests (to test neutron initiators and the effect of explosives on radioactive materials such as U-235 and plutonium tampers) which spread dangerous quantities of plutonium and cobalt-60 throughout the area. The indigenous community was displaced to a township at Yalata, although traditional people often wandered onto the restricted site and were exposed to radiation. In one case, a family of traditional aborigines walked through the test site and a woman later gave birth to a stillborn child. Four years later, her second child died at two of cancer. Yalata was a Lutheran mission where traditional knowledge was repressed and alcoholism and despair spread.[61]

At tests at Bikini Atoll in 1946 an entire indigenous community was dispossessed and dispersed into other parts of the Marshall Islands, where they are now vulnerable to rising sea levels from climate change.[62] US naval personnel were sent onto irradiated ships four days after one test. The first hydrogen bomb test, 'Mike', vaporized the island of Eugelab and exploded with a yield of 10.4 Mt. The 'Castle Bravo' test of 1954 had an unexpectedly powerful yield of 15 Mt and spread toxic radioactive fallout over a hundred miles of populated islands and a Japanese fishing vessel, the *Fukuryu Maru*, which was 220 km from ground zero. In total, 67 bombs were detonated on Enewetak and Bikini atolls between 1946 and 1958, equivalent to 1.6 Hiroshima bombs every day over the course of twelve years. After a half-hearted cleanup, contaminated topsoil and radioactive debris was placed in a 350 m crater and covered in a concrete dome on the island of Runit, which is now leaking into the surrounding ecosystem.[63]

In addition to tests in the Marshall Islands, the USA conducted some 86 atmospheric and 14 underground tests at the official test site in the southern Nevada desert. Nearby was the top-secret 'Area 51' – famous in UFO conspiracies and the *X-Files* TV series – which was used to test spy planes such as the U-2 and in 1957 hosted a secret 'dirty bomb' test where a plutonium weapon was crashed into the desert. Another 1957 thermonuclear test, code-named 'Hood', was (at 73 Kt) the largest explosion on US soil. It spread fallout over Area 51, shutting the base down for two years, and the blast wave was felt in Los Angeles.[64] These tests, including the notorious 'Sedan' test of 1962, spread fallout across Nevada, Utah, Arizona, Iowa, Nebraska, South Dakota and Illinois. The US government was eventually forced to disburse some $1.5 billion in compensation to cancer victims.[65]

France conducted 163 tests in French Polynesia between 1960 and 1996, showering the whole of the area in dangerous levels of fallout. In July 1974 one test blanketed Tahiti in airborne plutonium, subjecting its population to 500 times the allowed dose of radiation for two days.[66] Medical researchers have since found increased incidences of early onset cancer throughout the Marshall Islands and French Polynesia.[67] The Marshall Islands government accuses the USA of still owing funds from the $244 million awarded them by the Nuclear Claims Tribunal and in 2014 filed lawsuits in the US Federal Court and International Court of Justice suing the nuclear armed states for violating international law by failing to disarm.[68] Widespread controversy over France's persistence with testing in the Pacific also led to the infamous 1985 bombing of the Greenpeace vessel, the *Rainbow Warrior*, at port in Auckland by DGSE intelligence operatives. France later threatened trade sanctions against New Zealand if two of its agents convicted of the crime were not returned home.[69]

The USSR tested at Semipalatinsk, Kazakhstan, where between 1949 and 1989, 456 fission and thermonuclear devices were exploded, resulting in 'a number of genetic defects and illnesses in the region, ranging from cancers to impotency to birth defects and other deformities . . . as well as an epidemic of babies born with severe neurological and major bone deformations, some without limbs'. At one of the ten Soviet 'nuclear cities', Chelyabinsk-65, some seventy million cubic metres of radioactive waste was ejected into the Techa river, causing death, illness and deformities in the population of 124,000 who lived along its course.[70]

This chapter began by asking a fundamental question: how can nuclear weapons make an effective contribution to security? The narrative developed here suggests that they do the exact opposite: that while they have produced a terribly precarious form of 'national security' for the weapon states – one ever vulnerable to failures of deterrence, crisis instability and accidental nuclear war – they have only done so by threatening the very life of the planet. Nuclear strategies, however sophisticated, continually threatened to founder on their own contradictions. Every major technological advance made the system more unstable. Even the weapons at rest were dangerous, as Eric Schlosser demonstrates in his exploration of nuclear safety, *Command and Control*. At the centrepiece of that story of numerous weapons accidents is the toxic fuel leak and explosion of a 9 Mt Titan missile in its silo in Arkansas in September 1980. Had the warhead detonated, much of the state would have been devastated.[71] Furthermore, the nuclear production, testing and military complex produced grave and substantial harms to millions of people: military personnel forced on exercises in radioactive zones; civilians affected by waste, pollution and fallout; indigenous communities dispossessed from their ancestral lands and made sick with radiation; and damage to marine and riverine ecosystems. The humanitarian consequences agenda is a collective effort to remind the world of the more universal security needs – those of humanity and the planet – which remain threatened by the existence of nuclear weapons. Eliminating such weapons is both possible and politically and strategically complex. Chapter 6 considers the practical strategic thinking that has been advanced that could lead us closer to a nuclear weapons free world.

CHAPTER FOUR

Mining, Politics and People

It is one of the stranger ironies of the modern age that some of the most advanced scientific, industrial and military projects have come into direct confrontation with the world's oldest continuing human cultures.[1] Along with the experience of nuclear testing in the Pacific and South Australia, this confrontation has occurred most strongly in the mining of uranium. In the United States, Canada, Australia and Niger, in particular, indigenous peoples have worked in uranium mines, fought their establishment, brought lawsuits over their environmental and medical impacts and seen lands stolen by colonialism and war put to use for a new kind of militarism by state agencies just as disdainful of their historic rights and spiritual connection with the land. Similar impacts have also affected non-indigenous communities working and living around uranium mines and mills, sparking social and political conflict. Other major impacts from mining have been felt in the former Soviet Union, Namibia and South Africa. These struggles, which are ongoing, are an important document of nuclear harm and central to the politics of uranium.

This chapter is focused on a key fact: before uranium can be used it must be found beneath the earth's surface, recovered from the ground and milled into a form suitable for export. The exploration and mining process not only raises serious security concerns about the destination of supplies; it is a major global business, a business often pursued in politically and environmentally sensitive areas. Here the geopolitics of uranium takes on a different cast: it touches communities, especially indigenous communities, in their homelands and basic dignity. It raises complex and interrelated issues about land rights legislation, negotiation tactics, cultural heritage, environmental stewardship and regulation, the taxation of foreign investors and minerals companies and corporate and government power. Given that 70 per cent of global uranium deposits are located on the traditional lands of indigenous peoples, conflict over uranium is likely to continue.[2]

Table 4.1 Recoverable Resources of Uranium (as of January 2013)				
Country	Total Recoverable Resources (tU) Cost ranges <USD 130/kgU	Global distribution of Resources	Total production 2012 (tonnes U)	Total Production to 2012 (tonnes U)
Australia	1,706,100	29	7,009	183,239
Kazakhstan	679,300	12	21,240	199,413
Russian Federation	505,900	9	2,862	152,718
Canada	493,900	8	8,998	465,489
Niger	404,900	7	4,822	123,432
Namibia	382,800	6	4,653	113,323
South Africa	338,100	6	467	158,413
Brazil	276,100	5	326	3,925
United States	207,400	4	1,667	370,149
China	199,100	3	1,450	36,799
Mongolia	141,500	2		535
Ukraine	117,700	2	1,012	127,924
Uzbekistan	91,300	2	2,400	122,791
Botswana	68,800	1		
Tanzania	58,100	1		
Total	4,792,927	97	56,906	2,058,150

Source: OECD Nuclear Energy Agency and the International Atomic Energy Agency, Uranium 2014: Resources, Production and Demand, 2014, NEA no: 7209

This chapter surveys the uranium mining industry, setting out some of its history and current exploration and production trends related to industry demand. It also briefly explains the control regime that international society has developed around the export and sale of uranium to ensure – at least in theory – that it does not contribute to the proliferation and spread of nuclear weapons. (The recent US and Australian export deals with India have raised serious questions about the effectiveness of this regime, which is managed by the Nuclear Suppliers Group, or NSG.) However, the non-proliferation regime has no mechanisms to intervene in the more complex justice questions that arise from uranium mining as such and nor has it been able to grapple with the problem of nuclear waste or the lingering security and ecological concerns that it raises. Here the twin themes which structure this book – the material actancy of uranium as a substance and humanity's troubled effort to manage its dangers – converge to create profound questions of environmental justice and regulatory commitment.

The chapter then considers in more detail some of the legislative, human rights, environmental and land rights conflicts that have been associated with the mining of uranium both during the Cold War and more recently. It focuses on three major sites of conflict: mining in New Mexico and its impact on Navajo communities; the Ranger and Jabiluka mines in Australia's Kakadu National Park, which is both a World Heritage area and a recognized area of traditional Aboriginal ownership; and Canada, one of the world's largest producers, where Dené communities have sought compensation and exploration plans by the French uranium giant Areva in Nunavut have divided Inuit communities and aroused concerns about the environmental impact on caribou herds. It also touches on impacts felt by non-indigenous communities in the USA and Canada. One American anthropologist,

Barbara Rose Johnston, calls the groups affected by nuclear testing and mining 'radiogenic communities', communities 'produced by the process of radioactive decay ... people whose lives have been profoundly affected and altered by a hazardous, invisible threat, where the fear of nuclear contamination and the personal health and intergenerational effects of exposure color all aspects of social, cultural, economic and psychological well-being'.[3] While these radiogenic communities have included the white settlers (and mine and mill workers and families) of Arizona, Nevada, Utah and other downwind states, they disproportionally affect indigenous communities in North America, the South Pacific, Africa and Australia.

Uranium mining: a snapshot

In 2014 uranium was being mined and produced in twenty-one countries. Since 2009 the world's largest producer has been Kazakhstan, which produced 23,800 tonnes U in 2015, 39 per cent of world supply and nearly twice as much as the next largest, Canada (13,325 tonnes U in 2015, 22% of world supply). Australia is the world's third-largest producer (5672 tonnes U in 2015, 9%). The other major producers include Niger, Russia, Namibia, Uzbekistan, China and the United States. World uranium production currently supplies 90 per cent of world reactor requirements, with the remainder supplied by previously mined uranium including 'low enriched uranium (LEU) produced by blending down highly enriched uranium (HEU) from the dismantling of nuclear warheads, re-enrichment of depleted uranium tails (DU) and spent fuel reprocessing'.[4] The world's largest uranium mines were MacArthur River and Cigar Lake in Canada operated by Cameco (which produced respectively 12% and 7% of world totals) then Tortkuduk and Myunkum in Kazakhstan operated by Katko JV/Areva (7% of world production) and Olympic Dam in Australia operated by BHP Billiton (5% of world production). Kazatomprom (a state-owned Kazach firm) is the world's largest uranium miner, producing 21 per cent of world output, followed by Cameco (Canada) with 18 per cent, Areva (France) with 15 per cent and ARMZ-Uranium One (Russia) with 13 per cent. CNNC & CGN (China), BHP Billiton (UK-Australia) and Rio Tinto (UK-Australia) each control 5 per cent of world production.[5]

At the time of writing (mid-2016), uranium spot prices (per pound of U_3O_8 or 'yellowcake') were at near-historical lows of US$28, dropping from $40 at the beginning of 2015. Between 1970 and 2003 uranium prices were depressed ($5–20 a pound), especially during the 1990s as excess inventory from nuclear weapon stocks was diverted to civilian uses. Prices rose dramatically from 2004 peaking at $135 in 2007, but by 2010 had fallen back to $40. Prices rose again (to approximately $70) until the Fukushima disaster in 2011, after which Japan announced it was mothballing all of its nuclear power stations.[6] As it brings its plants back online it will use stockpiles accumulated after 2011 through existing purchase contracts. Projected growth in demand from China and India is expected to see prices stabilize at between $40 and $60 a pound to 2025, with some analysts suggesting that price recovery will not occur until 2018 or 2020.[7]

Because uranium fuel is a small element of the overall cost of nuclear energy, prices do not affect the construction of new power plants, but they do affect decisions about exploration and mine development. For example, after Australian Aboriginal traditional owners successfully vetoed the transport of uranium ore from Energy Resources Australia's Jabiluka site to the Ranger mill, Rio Tinto mothballed the new mine in 2001 as prices could not support the capital investment of a dedicated mill and yellowcake production facility.[8] The World Nuclear Association predicts that six new mines will go into production over the next decade: Husab (Namibia), Salamanca (Spain), Temrezli (Turkey), Mkuju River (Tanzania) and Mulga Rock and Wiluna (Australia). There exists nearly six million tons of recoverable terrestrial uranium (to US$130/pound), with Australia holding 29 per cent followed by Kazakhstan, Russia, Canada and Niger.[9] In short, 'peak uranium' is nowhere in sight and supplies of uranium have proven to be far more plentiful than Western leaders believed in the 1940s and 1950s. Long range strategic control over uranium deposits has been impossible.

Instead, three important sets of concerns around the mining and production of uranium have emerged. Firstly, the relatively easy availability of access to raw uranium has enabled the proliferation of nuclear weapons and necessitated the creation of control regimes around its export and sale. As the controversy over the US–India deal has shown, these regimes have significant flaws. Secondly, uranium mines create significant health risks to miners and local communities, who have historically been exposed to highly lethal levels of air- and water-borne radiation. Thirdly, mining activities have significant potential environmental impacts. They produce large amounts of contaminated radioactive and acidic waste rock (tailings) which must be stored and insulated from the surrounding environment, often in ponds, which creates the dangers of radiation exposure to the public or the release of contaminated water.

In-situ leaching techniques (sometimes called ISL or 'solution mining') are currently used to produce nearly 50 per cent of all uranium, primarily in Kazakhstan. They involve the injection of corrosive chemicals, via a groundwater bore, into a uranium deposit to dissolve the ore, which is then pumped back so that the uranium can be extracted. Wastewater is then injected back into underwater aquifers. Scientific critics of the method explain that the 'use of acidic solutions mobilizes high levels of heavy metals, such as cadmium, strontium, lead and chromium' while 'alkaline solutions tend to mobilize only a few heavy metals such as selenium and molybdenum'. They argue that 'the ISL technique merely treats groundwater as a sacrifice zone' and that 'ISL uranium mining is not controllable [and] is inherently unsafe'. Monash University's Gavin Mudd has argued that 'the use of sulphuric acid solutions at ISL mines across Eastern Europe, as well as a callous disregard for sensible environmental management, has led to many seriously contaminated sites . . . the most severe example is Straz pod Ralskem in the Czech Republic, where up to 200 billion litres of groundwater is contaminated. Restoration of the site is expected to take several decades or even centuries.'[10]

Controlling uranium sales and exports

The NPT prohibits non-nuclear member states from seeking to develop nuclear weapons themselves and, under Article III, from assisting other states in doing so. Article III of the treaty aims to prevent 'diversion of nuclear energy for peaceful uses to nuclear weapons or other nuclear explosive devices' and prohibits any state from providing fissionable material or 'equipment . . . designed for the processing, use or production of special fissionable material' unless the receiving state has concluded a safeguards agreement with the International Atomic Energy Agency (IAEA). These provisions have obvious application for the export of uranium, especially where they could be used directly for the production of nuclear weapons or otherwise free up domestic sources of uranium for weapons purposes.

These provisions of the NPT are enforced by a group of forty-eight nuclear supplier states called the Nuclear Suppliers

Group (NSG). The major world producers of uranium are all members, apart from Uzbekistan, Niger and Namibia. As well as enforcing the provisions of Article III, the NSG also forbids nuclear trade with countries which are not a party to the NPT and in full compliance with their obligations under the treaty. Nuclear trade is defined by a 'trigger list' of materials and technologies which includes: 'source material which means uranium containing a mixture of isotopes occurring in nature; uranium depleted in the isotope 235; thorium; or any of the foregoing the form of metal, alloy, chemical compound, or concentrate'.[11] These rules thus cover the export of semi-processed uranium ore in the form of yellowcake.

Controversy has arisen over agreements made with India which at least partially circumvent Article III of the NPT and the NSG guidelines. On 1 October 2008, the US Congress gave approval to an agreement between the USA and India on peaceful nuclear cooperation, which opened the door for the export of uranium and civilian nuclear technology including enrichment technology, nuclear energy plants and reactors. In November 2015 Australia and India also completed an agreement for bilateral nuclear trade which will open the door to the export of uranium and in 2013 Canada also completed an agreement with India. In April 2015 the Canadian uranium producer Cameco concluded a contract worth 350 million CAD to supply 7.1 million pounds of uranium concentrate to India's Department of Atomic Energy.[12]

Two key concerns have arisen. Firstly, India is a nuclear weapons state that is not a member of the NPT. It has a suspicious relationship with Pakistan with whom it has exchanged nuclear threats in the past and is modernizing its nuclear capabilities and delivery systems. It has also kept the door open to increasing the size of its nuclear arsenal. Hence the NSG rule prohibiting trade with non-NPT states has been waived, which undermines the non-proliferation regime by introducing a significant inconsistency and double standard. Secondly, it has also undermined Article III by only partially placing India's reactors and processing facilities under IAEA safeguards. Under the terms of the deal with the USA, India agreed to place fourteen of its twenty-two nuclear power reactors under permanent IAEA safeguards. However its military reactors remain unsafeguarded and it retains the sole prerogative to define future reactors as either civilian or military. Furthermore, all military facilities and stockpiles of nuclear fuel that were accumulated before the agreement remain exempt from inspections and safeguards, even though India has committed to working towards signing a Fissile Material Cut-off Treaty. This has been interpreted by Pakistan as creating greater freedom to divert existing stockpiles and future domestic production of uranium to military purposes. According to Mark Fitzpatrick of the International Institute for Strategic Studies, the deal has thus been strategically desta-bilizing. Pakistan is now leading international opposition to an FMCT and effectively blocking progress and introduced theatre nuclear weapons onto its defence doctrine in part as a response to India's favourable treatment.[13]

Indigenous peoples and mining

Just as the Cold War and post-war industrialization formed an enabling context for the proliferation of nuclear weapons and the growth of nuclear energy, colonialism forms a con-text for the encounter of indigenous peoples with uranium mining. The remainder of this chapter addresses three major examples where this has occurred, in the United States, Canada and Australia, while also touching on the experiences of non-indigenous communities. These, however, are not the only significant examples. During the Cold War, South Africa became the fourth largest uranium producer after the USA,

Canada and East Germany, although it was extracted as a byproduct of the mining of gold. The gold mining which occurred in South Africa from 1887 produced over 400 km² of tailings that included enormous amounts of radioactive uranium waste rock.[14] These have left an ongoing legacy. Over 600 abandoned mine sites surround Johannesburg, leaving slag piles close to residential communities. Winds blow toxic dust that includes copper, lead, cyanide and arsenic into people's homes and uranium leaches out of the tailings and abandoned mine sites into surrounding watercourses and wetlands.[15]

In Niger – a former French colony, the world's fourth-largest producer and one of the world's poorest countries – uranium mining has created severe tensions with the nomadic Tuareg people who live in the arid northwest of the country where uranium is found. In 2007–9 a Tuareg insurgent group, the MNJ, demanded a greater share of mining revenues from the French giant, Areva, and attacked Nigerien army garrisons, kidnapped Areva employees and a Chinese nuclear engineer, disrupted production and shipments and spread the conflict into Mali.[16] Areva operates a large open pit mine near Arlit and a deep underground mine near Akouta, towns built to service the remote operations. A third mine, Imouraren, is facing delays but may begin production in the 2020s. Areva's mines have produced some hundred thousand tonnes of uranium oxide throughout their life but until recently paid only 5.5 per cent in royalties to the Niger state ($111 million in 2010).[17] The government has since renegotiated the royalty agreements upwards to 12 per cent (dependent on profitability) for a five-year term beginning in 2014.[18] The Niger government has also granted exploration licences to Russia's Gazprom and two Indian companies, signed export agreements with South Korea and announced that it will let a further hundred exploration permits to build its uranium

industry and diversify investment beyond France.[19] This activity, however, could create further conflict with the Tuareg if
the profound environmental and health problems that typi-
fied Areva's mines are not addressed in new projects. Areva's
mines have left thirty-five million tonnes of uncovered tailings and 1600 tonnes of radioactive equipment and materials
(some of which were used by the community for housing
and utensils) and poor water management has contaminated
groundwater, wells and drinking water.[20]

In all these cases the colonization of these lands by
European powers and the establishment of settler-colonial
or post-colonial states opened the country to mining exploration and extraction and saw the State imposing powers and
rights over minerals that were rightly due to their indigenous
owners.[21] This has exposed indigenous and local communities to major cultural, health and ecosystem impacts, which
in many cases have been compounded by racist attitudes
that exposed them to comparatively greater levels of harm
and denied them natural justice as they sought to cope with
the after-effects. These practices of 'environmental racism'
have been termed 'wastelanding': a politics of land and space
'that renders an environment and the bodies that inhabit it
pollutable'.[22]

Analogous forms of wastelanding have also been practiced
on non-indigenous communities, such as those living in states
downwind from US nuclear test sites and in uranium mining
and milling towns as such Uranium City, Saskatchewan and
Monticello, Utah. The US Atomic Energy Commission conducted 100 atmospheric and underground nuclear tests in
Nevada from 1951 to 1992, all of which spread fallout across
Nevada, Utah and Arizona, with significant concentrations
also found in Colorado, Idaho, Montana and South Dakota.[23]
One historian, Howard Ball, argues that the AEC was aware
of the dangers of fallout but that 'when the AEC had to choose

between the necessity of atomic testing to maintain nuclear superiority over the Soviets and their serious concerns about radiation safety, conflicts were too often resolved in favor of the military's requirements'.[24] The AEC told downwind communities fallout was safe and suppressed early epidemiological studies of 1961 and 1963 that demonstrated links between fallout and increasing leukemia, thyroid and other cancers and highlighted the pathway to ingestion of iodine-131 and other radionuclides via fresh milk. The injustice prompted the formation of numerous citizens committees and congressional efforts (in 1979, 1981 and 1989) which culminated in the passage of the Radiation Exposure Compensation Act of 1990. After further citizen pressure it was amended in 2000 to extend the compensation from underground miners, immediate downwinders and test site personnel to surface miners, mill workers and ore transporters over a larger area downwind. Some $1 billion was paid under this law, but (as outlined below) families living in milling towns have been left to cover their enormous medical expenses alone.[25]

Monticello is one of a number of towns on the Colorado Plateau (including Moab, Nucla, Naturita and Uravan) built to service the Cold War uranium mining industry, house workers, and host milling plants. With a population of 1,958 people (83% white, 13% hispanic and 6% native American), the town hosted the Monticello Mill, which processed uranium and vanadium from 1942 to 1960 and created so much contamination that it hosted two US EPA 'Superfund sites' requiring $250 million in remediation. Until the EPA cleanup in the 1990s, the mill site contained two million tons of radioactive tailings, soil and building materials. Tailings dust blew through the town and into people's homes and waste rock was used in road and home building. The mill's operation also produced smokestack emissions from leaching agents like sulphuric acid. By the early 1990s the community became increasingly worried by cancer and respiratory illnesses. Surveys by the local community group VTME between 1993 and 2007 recorded 600 cases of cancer and 100 cases of respiratory illness (that is, 36% of the town's population). A 1997 Agency for Toxic Substances and Disease Registry (ATSDR) study noticed a 395 per cent increase in lung cancer deaths between 1950 and 1980 and an increase in breast cancer of 387 per cent for Caucasian women. Paying for medical treatment in the US system has burdened families with enormous medical bills, which the community was asking to be covered by a federal trust.[26]

The sociologist Stephanie Malin – who has extensively researched community attitudes and conflicts around the mill and Colorado Plateau mining – noted that the refusal of the ATSDR to link the illness definitively to the mill's presence angered Monticello residents, as did the fact that, even as by the mid-1950s US Public Health Service (PHS) studies revealed links between uranium exposure and cancer, the community was never warned. The lack of transparency about the study – with relevant records remaining classified or missing – has also angered locals. She quotes community members associating the disdain with which downwind communities were treated by the Atomic Energy Commission during atmospheric nuclear testing with their own treatment as victims of the milling operation. The VTME discovered an AEC memo written for scientists working at the test sites instructing them to delay detonations until winds were blowing towards southern Utah and northern Arizona, because they were inhabited by a 'low use segment of the population'. The community's ongoing nervousness about the mill's eventual remediation was increased by the fact that the entire town and mill at Uravan was demolished and its population moved out under the Superfund programme.[27] Malin analyses how the legacy of mining and milling in Monticello has been socially divisive, with some residents supporting and others opposing new planned facilities, in part because of a 'structural violence' produced by poverty and recession and dependence on the 'cyclonic' and unreliable patterns of resource development which depend on volatile commodities markets. The refusal by the federal government to acknowledge a link between the mill and cancer and to provide health costs has produced great bitterness: one local told her that 'so many people in this town are just so sad right now'.[28]

The United States: the Navajo on the Colorado Plateau
Uranium mining occurred extensively throughout Navajo lands across the 'four corners' area of the Colorado Plateau intersecting New Mexico, Colorado, Utah and Arizona from 1944 until 1986.[29] While uranium for the Manhattan Project was sourced from Canada and the Belgian Congo, the US Atomic Energy Commission (AEC) focused on the Four Corners area after 1939 as the key to developing a domestic supply. Native American knowledge of potential uranium deposits was highly sought after by prospectors, but their rights over their land and resources were not recognized. The Department of Interior let mining contracts – including a large contract to the Kerr-McGee Corporation in 1952 – and under the 1946 Atomic Energy Act the AEC controlled the uranium industry and required that all production be sold to it.[30]

Kerr-McGee hired 100 miners at only two-thirds the normal pay scale and some 300 to 500 additional Navajo also worked in smaller independent mining operations working shallower deposits. One rough estimate of the number of Navajo who worked in uranium mines puts the number at over 3000.[31] They worked in four main areas of mining and milling on reservation land near Shiprock New Mexico, Monument Valley Utah, Church Rock New Mexico and Kayenta Arizona. Many

Navajo also travelled off the reservation to work in mines, often taking their families with them and living in camps.[32]

Working conditions in the mines proved to be extraordinarily dangerous for both native and white American miners. The major danger derived from the decay products of radon gas ('radon daughters'). Radon is a noble gas produced by the decay of radium and is released into the atmosphere by blasting and drilling. It has a half-life of four days and decays into solid airborne particles (i.e. Radium A/Polonium-218, Radium C/Bismuth-214), which can be breathed into the lungs. The decay process works through thirteen elements and ends in Radium C (Polonium-210-lead). As one writer described it: 'If the disintegration cycle is completed, Polonium-210-lead with a half-life of twenty-two years, builds up in the body. Some of it is excreted. Much of it collects in the soft tissue and is eventually transmitted to the bone. Thus, the victim is being radiated from within his own body.'[33] Effective ventilation systems, which continually remove daughter-saturated air from shafts within two hours, can prevent radioactive particles from entering the body's DNA and creating long-term damage that leads to cancer.

However, ventilation systems were not installed in many mines, or were left turned off, and regulatory authorities failed to act even after they became aware of the dangers. Samples taken in 1950 at the Vanadium Corporation of America mine at Marysvale Utah measured 26,900 picocuries (pCi) of radon per litre of air, in comparison with the Public Health Service's estimate of 100 pCi as a safe level.[34] This 100 pCi level corresponds with what has been termed one 'working level', which is a measure of the energy released by radon daughters.[35] A 1957 report showed that radon concentrations in the majority of 157 mines tested 'were above levels that required ventilation'. Navajo miners worked in these conditions, ate their lunch inside the mineshafts, drank water from sources inside the mines, and returned home to their families in clothing coated in radioactive dust. In some mines, Navajo workers were forced to enter the mines filled with smoke and dust immediately after blasting, when white workers were not. Yet they were never told of the risk to their health from the radiation and, in what has been called an 'ethically troubling' protocol, US Public Health Service (PHS) scientists were only allowed to examine mine conditions and study worker health if they did not divulge their concerns to workers.[36] The PHS study uncovered a 'statistically significant association between uranium mining in lung cancer for white miners' and other epidemiological studies have uncovered strong links between Navajo workers' and communities' exposure to radiation and serious illness. Of the 150 Navajo miners who worked at the Shiprock mine, 38 had died of radiation induced cancer by 1980 and another 95 had contracted serious respiratory illness and cancers. Another review of medical records for the 13,329 Navajo born in the Shiprock area 'determined statistically significant associations between uranium exposure and unfavourable birth outcomes (such as miscarriages, cleft palates and other birth defects) when (a) the mother lived near tailings or mine dumps, (b) the father had a lengthy work tenure and (c) either parent worked in the Shiprock electronics assembly plant'. Thousands of Navajo and other native Americans in the Four Corners area also worked in milling operations and more general epidemiological studies of uranium millers have uncovered 'significant elevations' of certain non-malignant respiratory diseases and cancers.[37]

There has also been significant community exposure to mine tailings and contaminated groundwater and runoff. There are at least 900 abandoned mines and four mill sites on Navajo land, leaving an estimated 140 million tonnes of tailings and debris. Many tribespeople used radioactive waste rock for concrete and stone structures in their homes.

Children dug caves in mill tailings and played in the mines; communities drank invisibly contaminated water from pits that filled with rain; and they ate meat from their animals that drank from the same water.[38] At the uranium mine operated by United Nuclear Corporation (UNC) at Church Rock, New Mexico – the USA's largest – a failure in the earth tailings dam in July 1979 sent 1100 tons of radioactive mill waste and ninety-five million gallons of mine effluent into the Puerco River. Contaminants were transported 130 miles downstream and more radiation was released than at Three Mile Island. Pressure from UNC saw them allowed to resume operations in November, discharging waste water into unlined ponds leading to widespread groundwater contamination that saw the mill placed on the EPA's national priorities list in 1983. The request by the Navajo Tribal Council for McKinley County to be declared a disaster area was denied and the Centers for Disease Control declined to investigate exposure pathways such as consumption of vegetables or the ingestion of river or ground water, despite scientists identifying these as continuing concerns.[39]

Federal government responses have been fitful and inadequate. $240 million was spent to cover tailings piles at the mills, but the numerous mine sites were untouched. Other monies from a federal mine reclamation fund were used to block mine entrances and fill up pits. The Indian Health Service advised against action (or even surveys) of the contamination of homes 'due to the vast cost'. Meanwhile the US EPA conducted helicopter surveys of radiation on Navajo land and even made maps, but refused to share them with affected communities; Navajo environmental officials later ordered EPA surveyors off the reservation so they would not be inundated with tribal concerns for which there were no funds available. A 1982 lawsuit seeking $6.7 million from a federal claims court to seal and clean about 300 mines was dismissed, with the Navajo's claim 'that federal inspectors had failed to enforce safety standards in order to keep down the price of bomb material' rejected as 'entirely speculative'.[40] Historians, however, have uncovered documents showing that the AEC sought to suppress research into the dangers and ignored the results that scientists presented them with.[41]

This legacy of contamination, illness and official deceit has resulted in strong hostility to any new uranium mining projects on or close to Navajo land, reaching a flashpoint with the Nuclear Regulatory Commission's (NRC) grant of a licence to Hydro Resources Inc. (HRI) to perform in-situ leaching (ISL) uranium mining at four sites on Navajo land, near the communities of Church Rock and Crownpoint in McKinley County, New Mexico. The mines would be located in the Westwater Canyon aquifer, which supplies drinking water for 12,000 people, and one of the planned processing plants was to be close to the town of Crownpoint and within half a mile of churches, businesses, schools, government offices and residential areas. The NRC approved the company's environmental impact statement in February 1997 and their mining application in January 1998, despite scientific testimony that uranium leaching would contaminate the aquifer. Navajo organizations responded by filing numerous briefs challenging the NRC's findings and the safety of the project.

In 2005 Navajo nation president Joe Shirley Jr signed the Diné Natural Resources Protection Act which prohibited all uranium mining within Navajo Indian country, blocking development of further mines on an estimated 25 per cent of US uranium reserves. The president stated that while 'there are no answers to cancer, we shouldn't have uranium mining on the Navajo nation ... [the government has] committed genocide on Navajo land by allowing uranium mining'. The act also amended Title 18 of the Navajo Nation Code (the Navajo constitution), which now states that 'no person shall engage in uranium mining or uranium processing on any sites within Navajo country'.[42] Since then, the Navajo have energetically sought to thwart the HRI project getting under way. They unsuccessfully appealed the NRC's approval through to the US Supreme Court in 2010 and in 2011 submitted a petition to the Inter-American Commission on Human Rights.[43] Despite HRI efforts to divide the community and circumvent the Diné ban on mining, as of 2014 they had been unable to start the project.[44]

Canada: the Dené of the Northwest Territories
Canada is the world's second largest producer of uranium. It has been a major source dating from the Second World War, when the mine at Port Radium on the Great Bear Lake in the Northwest Territories was repurposed to extract uranium which was sent to the United States for the Manhattan Project. Uranium was mined at Port Radium from 1942 after contracts were let by the US government to the Canadian Crown Corporation Eldorado Mining and Exploration. Great Bear Lake is the ancestral land of the Dené indigenous community which has fished the lake and lived off caribou herds for tens of thousands of years. Some 800 Dené lived in the township of Déline and travelled widely across the lake and associated lands hunting and fishing. Despite the Dené having ancestral rights to the land – which were not recognized by the Canadian Supreme Court until 1973 – when radium was first discovered in 1930, they received a few sacks of flour, lard and baking powder in exchange for the rights to extract an exotic mineral then worth $70,000 a gram on world markets.[45]

It is not believed that Dené men from Déline worked within the mine, but from the 1930s until 1960 they were used as labour to transport uranium ore south to Fort McMurray, along a 2,100 km route of lakes, roads and rivers known as 'the highway of the atom'. They piloted the barges and carried 45 kg gunny sacks of crushed uranium ore on their backs to load onto barges and trucks, which often spilled. Their families camped by the lake near the mine during the summers. Journalist Andrew Nikiforuk has described how community members 'ate fish from contaminated dredging ponds. Their children played with the dusty ore at river docks and portage landings. And their women sewed tents from used uranium sacks.'[46] The mine superintendent built a sandbox at Port Radium's school out of fine ground uranium tailings and white miners worked in shafts thick with radon, which were ventilated only by natural circulation. The closure of the mine in 1960 left behind some 1.7 million tonnes of tailings (800,000 tonnes in the lake itself) emitting elevated levels of gamma radiation. They remain in the path of periodic caribou migration, which is a major source of meat for the Inuit. The animals walk on the tailings, eat lichens growing there and drink from the contaminated lake water.[47]

The health impacts of the mine both on the Dené community and white miners have been a source of bitterness and conflict. By 1998 some 14 Déline men (nearly half those who worked transporting the crushed ore) had died of cancer. The community issued a 14-point declaration and a 106-page report based on their own research and demanded a meeting with the Bureau of Indian Affairs and the Minister for Resources in Ottawa.[48] Two years later a joint Dené-Canadian government committee was formed called the Canada-Déline Uranium Table (CDUT) to investigate the human health and environmental impacts of Port Radium. However its final 2005 report was far from the 'comprehensive health, environmental and social assessment' that the Dené had demanded. The study narrowly focused on mortality rather than exposure and even after it was estimated that given 'risk modelling based on the dose reconstruction, 1.6 excess cancers (more than baseline) are theoretically predicted in a group of thirty-five individuals with ages and radioactive doses the same as the transport workers', stated that there was no conclusive evidence that uranium transport workers experienced any direct health impacts from radiation exposure.[49] The report failed to account for the cultural impacts of the deaths: chair of the Déline Uranium Committee Cindy Gilday told Andrew Nikiforuk that 'in Dené society it is the grandfather who passes on the traditions and now there are too many men with no uncles, fathers or grandfathers to advise them . . . [it is] cultural genocide . . . and its in my own home.'[50]

Nikiforuk documented sustained efforts on the part of the Canadian government to suppress knowledge about the damaging health effects of radiation and conceal it from mine workers and communities. In 1932 Canada's Department of Mines conducted studies of Port Radium which showed awareness of the dangers of radon and 'from inhalation of radioactive dust'. Ten years later a scientist from the US National Cancer Institute, Wilhelm C. Hueper, reviewed 300 years of radon data from European miners and warned that 'in case the Belgian and Canadian operations should be conducted without the essential and comprehensive protective measures for the workers, the prospects for an epidemic-like appearance of lung carcinomas among their employees can be anticipated in the not too distant future'. However in 1949 the US Atomic Energy Commission, then the major purchaser of Canadian uranium, ordered that information about the dangers 'not be quoted in any published report'. A 1953 study of Port Radium's sister mine on Lake Athabasca was initially printed, declassified and distributed; however every copy was recalled and hidden away at the request of Eldorado Mining. In 1959 Canada's energy minister, Gordon Churchill, claimed that 'there are no special hazards attached to the mining of uranium that differ from other mining activities'.[51]

The 1998 report and declaration issued by the Dené Uranium Committee after extensive community consultation, *They Never Told Us These Things*, demanded an immediate environmental cleanup, the containment and removal of uranium waste, compensation for the widows of men who had died of cancer and renegotiation of treaties that included contaminated land.[52] The Canadian government responded with a three-point plan focused on the health study and mine remediation.[53] They cancelled tickets for members of the Dené delegation and lawyers who assisted the Dené in their meetings with Ottawa spoke of the delaying tactics being used: 'they are trying to get you so tired and so frustrated and so unhappy that you just go back and you just give up'.[54] Especially sinister has been the sealing of Eldorado's records after its 1988 privatization and merger with Saskatchewan Mining Development Corporation to create the mining giant, Cameco. The records became property of the subsidiary, Canada Eldor, and in 2004 their status became 'closed' just as the CDUT was conducting their environmental and health investigation on behalf of Déline and the Canadian government.[55]

Other aspects of the Dené story are striking and moving, exemplifying the significance of indigenous spirituality and philosophy. From the 1940s on, one of the Dené 'grandfathers' and 'great aboriginal seers', Louis Ayah, warned that the waters of Great Bear Lake would be contaminated with a yellow poison that would flow towards the village. A female elder said of him: 'the prophet spoke about that poison. He said that there would be sickness and that people would go through hard times and that there would be deaths'. Another ancient Dené prohibition had held that:

> it was bad medicine to travel in front of the area now known as Port Radium; it was said that loud noises came from within it. For some reason a group of hunters had camped there and in the morning the medicine man told them of

his dream, in which he saw white people going into a large hole in the ground with machines. He saw boats on the lake and huge flying birds loaded with things. They were making something long, like a stick, that they dropped on people, burning everyone.[56]

In the 1990s, when the Déline community became aware of the history of Port Radium and the fact that it had delivered uranium to the bombs that were used to end the Pacific War, it organized a delegation to travel to Hiroshima to apologize to the victims and acknowledge their responsibility. No one from Cameco or the Canadian government travelled with them; the delegation was made up solely of members of a First Nation, some of whom had never travelled abroad, who wanted to draw a cosmic circle between the events and connect their two communities in a shared discourse of mourning and experience. Cultural theorists and philosophers are aware of the radically different idea of responsibility that was enacted here. Whereas Western ethics focus merely on the intentions of individuals and distances them from the systemic or historical impacts of their actions and experience, it seemed natural to the Dené to understand and act on their part in the causal chain, to see their experience as part of a larger moral and historical web. When the ethnographer Peter van Wyck asked the Dené why they had gone to meet the Hibakusha, they simply told him it was 'because it seemed like the right thing to do . . . in fact, my interest in asking the question to begin with was seen as a bit odd'.[57]

This history, as well as concern about the environmental and cultural impact of uranium mining, continues to complicate exploration and development plans in Canada's multi-billion dollar uranium industry. Some 44 different companies have prospected in the Northwest Territories and Nunavut since 2000, including on Dené land. While the Déline Land Corporation stated that it would oppose all uranium development until issues with Port Radium were resolved, it approved the Eldorado South IOCG & uranium project. At another site, Screech Lake, the Mackenzie Valley Environmental Review Board determined that Ur Energy's plans for exploration would 'cause adverse cultural impacts of a cumulative nature to areas of very high spiritual significance to Aboriginal peoples' and rejected the application. The Lutselk'e Dene First Nation of the Northwest Territories was strongly opposed to uranium mining. The province of British Columbia imposed a ban on uranium exploration in 2008 and has been sued by International Montoro Resources Inc. for damages. In 2013 Québec announced a moratorium on all uranium development and in 2015 was sued by Strateco Resources for CAD190 million for losses from the Matoush project after it was refused licences for the underground exploration phase, a project strongly opposed by the Cree Nation of Mistissini.[58] In Nova Scotia, a 1981 moratorium on uranium exploration was legislated into a ban in 2009 and in Ontario new laws required mining companies to consult with aboriginal communities at an early phase of the project. In Nunavut, where indigenous communities have been more supportive of uranium development, the government declared a policy that it would approve projects if the uranium mined is 'used only for peaceful and environmentally responsible purposes', that high health, safety and environmental standards are upheld, and that 'Nunavummiut must be the major beneficiaries of uranium exploration and mining activities', which should only continue if they have the support of affected Nunavummiut communities.[59]

Australia: the Mirarr-Gundjeihmi of Kakadu

Australian aboriginal peoples have long been impacted by the nuclear industry. In the 1950s the British government tested nuclear weapons on aboriginal lands at Maralinga, resulting in widespread contamination and a payment of \$13.5 million to the Maralinga Tjarutja people. Major Australian uranium mines include Rio Tinto's Ranger mine, built on the lands of the Mirarr-Gundjeihmi clan in Kakadu National Park (which at its peak was producing 6% of world output), and BHP Billiton's Olympic Dam project, built on the lands of the Kokatha clan of northern South Australia (which in 2015 produced 5% of world output). A highly controversial proposal to mine another rich ore body on Mirarr land, Jabiluka, provoked an eight-month blockade by activists, two parliamentary enquiries and a UNESCO investigation, and is discussed below. Two smaller mines, Beverley/Four Mile, operate 550 km north of Adelaide in South Australia on Adnyamathanha land. Radium was mined at Radium Hill and Mount Painter in South Australia in the 1930s and between 1950 and 1971 uranium was produced at Mary Kathleen in Queensland, Rum Jungle in the Northern Territory, and Radium Hill. This uranium was directed primarily at US and UK weapons programmes but was also sold to electricity producers.[60]

The Beverley/Four Mile deposits are extracted through in-situ leaching (ISL) methods and are relatively small. The Beverley ore bodies ceased production in 2014 and Four Mile produced 922 tonnes U_3O_8 in 2014–15 (a third that of Olympic Dam). The project went forward with the agreement of the native title claimants (who do not have a right of refusal under national native title law, unlike projects which fall under the Northern Territory Land Rights Act) but the approval has been criticized. There are divisions within the Aboriginal community over the mine, with a group of Adnyamathanha people continuing to oppose the development through the Flinders Ranges Aboriginal Heritage Consultative Committee, raising concerns about the potential pollution of water tables by the ISL process, a lack of career paths for aboriginal workers and the impact on the area's spiritual values.[61] In 2002 Jillian Marsh, an Adnyamathanha community member and researcher, told a Senate Inquiry 'that Heathgate's initial negotiations with the Adnyamathanha people, before the official opening of the Beverley mine in 2001, was "misrepresentative, ill-informed and designed to divide and disempower the community".'[62] The Four Mile project – an expansion of the existing lease – was also approved in 2009 by the Commonwealth Minister for the Environment on the basis of a Public Environment Report (PER), a less rigorous process than a full Environmental Impact Assessment (EIS). That minister was the former Midnight Oil singer Peter Garrett, whose band had played to protesters at the Jabiluka blockade.

A new proposed open pit mining project, Yeelirrie, operated by Cameco near Wiluna and 400 km north of the Western Australian goldfields town of Kalgoorlie, has run into trouble. At full production the project would be the largest in Australia (with planned exports of up to 7500 tonnes of U_3O_8 annually), but it has been strongly opposed by local aborigines and, at the time of writing, had failed to win approval from Western Australia's Environmental Protection Agency because of a concern about damage to subterranean fauna. A final decision now rests with the State and Commonwealth governments.[63]

Rio Tinto's Ranger mine in the Northern Territory is built on the lands of the Mirarr-Gundjeihmi people and lies inside the Kakadu National Park, a rich tropical mosaic of ecosystems with extraordinary biodiversity and numerous sites of spiritual significance dating back to the earliest human habitation of Australia 50,000 years ago. It contains 7000 rock art sites, 900 plant species, one-third of Australia's bird species, one-quarter of its freshwater fish, 21 of its 29 mangrove species and 100 species of amphibians and reptiles.[64] Between 1981 and 1992 Kakadu was also inscribed on UNESCO's World Heritage List for both its natural and cultural values, but the Ranger and Jabiluka mines have been legally excised from Kakadu National Park even as their environmental and cultural impacts on the park have been matters of intense scrutiny, protest and controversy.[65] The area is also subject to the Northern Territory Aboriginal Land Rights Act of 1979, a fact that has made relations with aboriginal people particularly important and fraught.

Uranium was discovered at Ranger in 1971 and in 1976 the mine was approved by the Commonwealth in the face of opposition from then Senior Traditional Owner, Toby Gangali. Even though the Aboriginal Land Rights (Northern Territory) Act was legislated the same year and provides traditional owners the right to negotiate and refuse development on their land, it included a clause that protected Pancontinental Mining from having to negotiate with aborigines once they had made a successful land claim.[66] Ranger (and Jabiluka) are now owned and operated by Energy Resources Australia (ERA), a 68 per cent owned subsidiary of the global resources giant Rio Tinto. It began production in 1981 and in 2010 the mine was the world's second largest source of uranium. Mining of the open pit ceased in 2013 and it has since been selling processed stockpiled ore (some 2000 tonnes per year). At the time of writing, Ranger's future, both in terms of production and rehabilitation, was in some doubt. ERA has spent $177 million developing access to an underground deposit within the mine boundaries called Ranger Deeps 3. However it has deferred plans to exploit the deposit because of both depressed uranium prices and the requirement to cease operations in 2021 when its authority expires. After the expiry of its authority, ERA is required to decommission the mine and spend hundreds of millions rehabilitating the site, including the disposal of millions of tonnes of tailings. However, ERA has posted over $900 million in pre-tax losses since 2010 and seen a dramatic drop in its share price, raising concerns about whether its rehabilitation liability will be funded given that the Commonwealth holds only a $60 million bond and Rio Tinto has verbally distanced itself from responsibility.[67] The traditional owners have opposed the Ranger Deeps concept, saying that 'as things stand today we will not support any extended term of mining at Ranger beyond 2021. We take this position because of our experience of thirty years of environmental and cultural impacts at Ranger and because in our talks with Rio Tinto and the Australian Government we have been given no guarantee that Ranger will be the last uranium mine in Kakadu'.[68]

Long-term environmental, cultural and moral legacies of the decision to mine Ranger are of declared concern to the Mirarr. In a way that echoes the decision of the Dené to visit Hiroshima, the Gundjeihmi Aboriginal Corporation explains that 'as traditional landowners, the Mirarr bear responsibility for the impacts that activity on their land has on others. The possibility of uranium from Mirarr land being incorporated into a nuclear weapon or present at the site of a nuclear accident is therefore of enormous concern to Mirarr.' In April 2011, after the Japanese tsunami, Senior Traditional Owner Yvonne Margarula wrote to UN Secretary-General Ban Ki-Moon and 'expressed her sorrow at the impacts radiation is having on the lives of Japanese people'. She wrote that, 'it is likely that the radiation problems at Fukushima are, at least in part, fuelled by uranium derived from our traditional lands. This makes us feel very sad.'[69]

The 2002 Senate Inquiry into uranium mining regulation listed 178 environmental incidents at Ranger – comprising numerous 'leaks, spills, accidents and poor performance' – but the Supervising Scientist (an office legislated to monitor environmental issues raised by the mine) insisted that they have had no significant ecological impact.[70] ERA has been accused of 'major delays in reporting incidents to stakeholders and regulators'[71] and incidents have included the use of tailings water to fight bushfires, run-off into Kakadu National Park from the high-grade ore stockpile (1994), a 12,000 litre diesel spill which killed forty waterbirds (1995), a failure of the tailings pipeline which discharged 85,000 litres of contaminated water into wetlands (2000) and four years of wet season flooding from the tailings ponds into Kakadu National Park (1998–2001).[72] In December 2013, there was a catastrophic failure of a leach tank which spilled one million litres (1,400 cubic metres) of acidic uranium slurry into the mine site. A similar tank had failed a week before at Rio Tinto's mine in Namibia.[73] A report by the supervising scientist stated that the spill 'has not resulted in any adverse impacts to human health or the surrounding environment' but conceded that limited groundwater analysis had been undertaken and that 'a small volume of contaminants may have entered the groundwater'. It recommended an increase in the frequency and intensity of groundwater monitoring in the region and further investigation of groundwater structures and movement.[74] This recommendation came more than a decade after a Senate enquiry had recommended similar investigations because of concerns that uranium had seeped 'from tailings dams via fault zones into shallow and deep aquifers'.[75] A 2006 survey by the Australian Institute of Aboriginal and Torres Strait Islander Studies suggested that the incidence of cancer (27 cases) in the Kakadu region was twice as high as rates for aborigines across the Northern Territory and recommended further investigation.[76] The Mirarr now have representation on the Ranger mine site technical committee which oversees environmental matters, after years of being excluded and concerns repeated in three separate parliamentary enquiries that the supervising scientist was insufficiently independent from ERA or government and that systems for environmental regulation were confusing and ineffective.[77]

Bitterness between the Mirarr and ERA was deepened further by the experience of ERA's efforts to develop the Jabiluka deposit, which is 20 km north of Ranger and contains as much uranium in higher concentrations. The development of Jabiluka was initially prevented by the election of a Labour government in 1983, which refused to approve new uranium mines, but became possible once a Conservative government was elected in 1996. Two aspects of the project – negotiations with Aborigines and government approvals – were especially controversial. Local traditional owners claimed that the original 1982 agreement with Pancontinental was coerced, because the Senior Traditional Owner had been subject to a campaign of inducements and exhaustion and the Northern Land Council (which is granted the responsibility to negotiate for aborigines under the Northern Territory Land Rights Act) failed to represent their interests properly. The 1999 Senate Inquiry into the Jabiluka project pointed to the irony that 'the provisions of the Land Rights Act, in which Traditional Owners are not parties to contracts negotiated on their behalf, already create scope for those rights to be unfairly alienated within contracts which may otherwise be technically legal'.[78]

The Mirarr Senior Traditional Owner, Yvonne Margarula, refused to agree to a radically new site proposal in 1996 and maintained that her father's 'agreement was obtained under duress and that before his death he beseeched her to prevent the mine's development and to protect the Boiwek-Almudj [sacred] sites'. She undertook extensive legal action in the Northern Territory Supreme Court, the Federal Court and the High Court, in an effort to prevent the mine from going ahead.[79] However the Australian government approved the revised proposals, ignoring the objections of the traditional owners and numerous concerns in its own departmental environmental assessments about cultural impacts, radiation and tailings management.[80] In 1998 Yvonne Margarula was arrested for trespassing on the mine site – that is, *on her own land* – along with 500 others during an eight-month long blockade by some five thousand activists. The traditional owners also petitioned the World Heritage Committee and the 1999 Senate Inquiry recommended that the mine not proceed. This opposition took place against a profound historical and contemporary background of aboriginal cultural decline, losses and struggle: the enquiry noted anthropological studies which recorded Kakadu's aboriginal population falling from 2,000 pre-contact to fewer than one hundred in 1980, the loss of numerous languages and efforts to rebuild aboriginal life and spirituality in the region free from the influence of development and alcohol. A statement issued by the Gundjeihmi Aboriginal Corporation on behalf of the Mirarr Gundjeihmi, Mirarr Erre, Bunitj and Manilakarr clan leaders said, 'a new mine will make our future worthless and destroy more of our country . . . Our future depends on our culture remaining strong. It is important for our obligations to each other to be recognized and our responsibilities to country to be met. Our cultural values cannot be traded for money.'[81]

A fall in world prices kept the mine in mothballs for a decade, because the Mirarr had refused to grant consent for the trucking of ore across their land from Jabiluka to the mill at Ranger and depressed world prices made the construction of a dedicated mill at Jabiluka unprofitable. In 2005 ERA signed the *Jabiluka Long-Term Care and Maintenance Agreement* with the Mirarr and the Northern Land Council and stated that 'while the Jabiluka Mineral Lease and the 1982 Jabiluka Mining Agreement remain in force, the [agreement] obliges ERA (and its successors) to secure Mirarr consent prior to any future mining development of uranium deposits at Jabiluka'.[82] Even as the company buried 50,000 tonnes of unprocessed ore back into the mine tunnel, renewed pressure was placed on the Mirarr to permit the mine to go ahead

during 2006 native title negotiations over the town of Jabiru
and in 2007 Rio Tinto executives indicated their hopes that
they could persuade Yvonne Margarula to relinquish her
opposition.[83] Hence, the Mirarr may well face new pressures in future to agree to Jabiluka's development. As the
Gundjeihmi Aboriginal Corporation puts it, the conflict has
been 'quarantined', but not ended.[84]

Conclusion

With world uranium oxide production in 2015 worth approximately $6.2 billion,[85] uranium mining is big business with
high stakes. However this chapter has shown that it is also a
business with profound social and environmental costs and
political and strategic complexities. On the one hand, indigenous and other communities have suffered profound health,
ecological and social impacts from uranium mining on their
land, many of which have not been adequately compensated
or resolved; on the other, mining companies have often lost
millions of dollars of investment after underestimating the
resolve and power of indigenous communities to oppose their
projects – especially when they combine with national and
international organizations and activist groups. In Canada
and Australia, huge and potentially lucrative deposits of uranium remain off-limits to mining because of community
opposition and, as the Jabiluka case showed, even when the
political and legal ground is tilted heavily towards miners,
they can still lose. Whereas mining during the Cold War was
subject to few controls and responsibilities, mining nowadays
requires compliance with far more stringent health and environmental standards and consideration of the interests of local
and indigenous communities. And when those standards fall
short, international scrutiny and publicity is not far away. The
significance of this agenda was exemplified by the OECD and

the Nuclear Energy Agency producing a joint report in 2014 setting out corporate and regulatory best practice in uranium mining.[86]

An important lesson from this history is that, when developing projects and conducting operations, mining corporations must respect the wishes of traditional owners and consider the interests and voices of indigenous and other local communities. They must incorporate these responsibilities and costs into their business planning, rather than seek to lobby their way around them. Governments likewise need to respect aboriginal land rights and create legislative and regulatory frameworks that ensure the protection of vulnerable ecosystems and respect for community rights of veto and negotiation. Indigenous communities are divided about the value of mining on their land – in some cases valuing the employment and development opportunities it provides and in others believing the cultural and environmental costs to be too great – and their views and prior ownership of the land should be respected more faithfully. When the experience of indigenous peoples with nuclear testing is considered alongside their experience with mining, it is clear that they have been asked to bear a grossly unjust and inordinate burden of the nuclear age.

CHAPTER FIVE

Energy, Risk and Climate

Climate scientists have now reached a strong consensus that increases in average global temperatures must be limited to at least two degrees celsius (and more safely, 1.5°C) to avoid dangerous levels of anthropogenic climate change.[1] Current global emissions trends suggest that limiting increases to this level could be very difficult and even the voluntary pledges made by governments at the historic 2015 Paris agreement on climate change were acknowledged, within its very text, to be inadequate.[2] 'Business-as-usual' projections of global greenhouse emissions, which assume no or modest efforts at reduction, show average global temperatures rising by 3–4° by the end of this century – a scenario that would subsequently see melted ice caps, many metres of sea level increase, flooded coastal cities and island states, massive ocean biodiversity loss, more intense tropical cyclones, and the destruction of the Amazon as a tropical ecosystem.[3] The Paris pledges would still see the Earth warm by 2–3.5°C.[4] With electrical energy emissions supplying approximately 25 per cent of global totals, nuclear power has assumed a new importance in plans for states to reduce their emissions and for global efforts at climate change mitigation.[5] Emissions reductions that can restrain global warming within safe boundaries require a near-zero-carbon world by 2050.

With the looming climate crisis in the background, this chapter considers some key policy and political questions raised by nuclear power and tries to avoid the very polarized positions taken respectively by the pro-nuclear lobby and anti-nuclear environmentalists. Nuclear energy has a value that environmentalists often downplay but also has serious social and environmental costs and risks that the nuclear lobby also downplays. The chapter looks at the uncertainties around future growth patterns in nuclear energy and invest-ment, the challenges raised by the nature and age of the technology, the challenges of nuclear waste disposal and secu-rity and, in the wake of Chernobyl and Fukushima, the issue of safety and the related problem of appropriate regulation and oversight. It argues that, given the enormous economic, environmental and social damage that (even very rare) nuclear accidents can do, there is value in considering a more strin-gent international regime to regulate the civilian nuclear industry and insure safety, rather than leaving the task to states alone.

The nuclear power industry and the use of nuclear energy for other 'peaceful uses' began to expand after US President Eisenhower addressed the United Nations General Assembly in December 1953. In what became known as the 'atoms for peace speech', he argued that the promotion of the peaceful uses of nuclear energy should be combined with efforts to slow and reverse the arms race. 'It is not enough to take this weapon out of the hands of the soldiers', he told the listen-ing diplomats. 'It must be put into the hands of those who will know how to strip its military casing and adapt it to the arts of peace.' He laid out his hope for 'the day when fear of the atom will begin to disappear from the minds of the people and the governments of the East and West' and proposed the creation of a common stock of fissionable material and a new agency under the aegis of the United Nations – which became the International Atomic Energy Agency (IAEA) – with a special responsibility to 'devise methods whereby this fissionable material would be allocated to serve the peaceful

pursuits of mankind'.[6] While the nuclear arms race accelerated, the idea of atoms for peace became entrenched in the
nuclear non-proliferation regime as a sovereign privilege of
state signatories to the NPT which affirmed (in Article IV)
'the inalienable right of all the Parties to the Treaty to develop
research, production and use of nuclear energy for peaceful
purposes'.[7] The complications this has caused in restraining
weapons proliferation have been raised in previous chapters
and will be taken up again in Chapter 6; however, the safety
and environmental challenges that nuclear energy has posed
in the large-scale supply of electricity were not anticipated in
the technological optimism that surrounded Eisenhower's
speech and the establishment of the IAEA. Nuclear power
now presents the world with a more mixed and complex
picture.

Decarbonization and nuclear power

The nuclear power industry has taken an active presence at
major international meetings such as Kyoto, Copenhagen and
Paris, in part to (unsuccessfully) counter lobbying by environmental NGOs and some governments against the inclusion
of nuclear energy in international market mechanisms.[8]
The nuclear energy industry has thus begun to speak of a
'nuclear renaissance' and actively promote nuclear power
as a solution to climate change, increasing energy demand
and strategic concerns about national dependence on oil and
other fossil fuels. The World Nuclear Association (WNA)
states that 61 reactors with 64 gigawatts (GWe) of capacity
are presently under construction and estimates that another
170 reactors (178 GWe) may come online during the next
ten years and that 339 are in the planning stage (381 GWe).
Projected expansion is highest in China, India, Russia and
Europe.[9]

The International Atomic Energy Agency (IAEA) is promoting growth in nuclear power generation as part of the solution to climate change and the World Nuclear Association was present at the Paris meeting of the UNFCC, where its Director General, Agneta Rising, said that 'the nuclear industry stands ready to deliver more to help tackle climate change. Nuclear generation could provide 25 per cent of the world's electricity with low carbon generation by having 1,000 gigawatts of new build by 2050.'[10]

The WNA's projection of 1,000 GWe of new nuclear energy capacity by 2050 is an optimistic one. At the end of 2014 there were 438 nuclear power reactors in operation with a total capacity of 376 GWe and IAEA projections for 2050 range from a low case of less than 400 GWe – that is, unchanged in total but with more in East Asia and less in Europe and the USA – and a high case of about 950 GWe in 2050. The IAEA explains that its lower projection 'reflect[s] national responses to the Fukushima Daiichi accident . . . [which] include earlier than anticipated reactor retirements, delayed or possibly cancelled new builds and increased costs owing to changing regulatory requirements'.[11] To these factors we should also add the problem of financing, which is touched on below.

The IAEA estimates that nuclear energy has avoided emissions of 64.5 Gt CO_2 from 1971 to 2012 (approximately 6% of total greenhouse emissions for the period) and that in a scenario in which global warming is stabilized at 2°C by 2050, nuclear power capacity will double to 862 GWe by 2040 and increase its share of global generation from 12 to 18 per cent (with renewables increasing from 21% to 51% and fossil fuels falling from 61% to 30%).[12] This larger projection would avoid 1.5 billion tonnes of carbon emissions annually.[13] The 'Nuclear for Climate' group also argues that low emissions electricity can replace fossil fuels in many other sectors, including domestic heating and transport, thus making an even larger contribution to climate change mitigation, which is a position reflected by the IAEA.[14]

Decarbonizing the world economy is an imperative for planet Earth's survival and an unalloyed good. This arguably implies that we should accept and manage the risks associated with nuclear energy, given the contribution that it can make to reducing emissions. However it is not a fully renewable or sustainable energy source, even if, according to the IAEA, 'nuclear power plants produce virtually no greenhouse gas emissions or air pollutants during their operation and only very low emissions over their entire life cycle'. The IAEA has compared the life cycle emissions of various fossil fuel and renewable energy sources and concluded that nuclear is generally comparable to (and often lower than) solar, wind and hydropower.[15] Nuclear power has no immediate greenhouse or other toxic emissions and is thus strongly preferable to coal- and gas-fired electricity generation.

However, nuclear power also comes with a range of complications and drawbacks. Once nuclear fuel is used up, nuclear power generation creates a substantial amount of highly radioactive isotopes as waste ('high-level waste' or HLW) which must be stored and cooled for many years and in turn either must be reprocessed (which creates liquid HLW) and/ or vitrified into casks which will be stored securely away for thousands of years in geological waste repositories – none of which have yet opened. Waste issues are discussed further below, but even as reliable technological solutions are available, the storage and security challenges should not be underestimated. Many established nuclear power plants are moving towards the end of their life and as they age create maintenance and safety challenges; conversely, new investment is economically challenging. New nuclear investments are extraordinarily expensive and generally require loan and price guarantees and other subsidies from government. As part of a climate change mitigation strategy, they would only make sense as part of a more general and concerted effort to support all forms of renewable energy investment, eliminate fossil fuel subsidies and rapidly phase out coal- and gas-fired power. So far, few governments have outlined such strategies.

One telling example is the problematic effort by the UK government to establish two new pressurized water (EPR) reactors at Hinkley Point in Somerset, using private investment. They are intended to have a very large capacity of 3.2 GWe and supply 7 per cent of the UK's electricity. The project partners are France's EDF and the China General Nuclear Corporation (CGN) with respective holdings of 66.5 per cent and 33.5 per cent, but it was expected that CGN would eventually increase its holding to near 50 per cent given that EDF was carrying high levels of debt and had been threatened with a downgrade in its credit rating if the project went ahead. The plant was originally projected to cost £16 billion in 2013 and cost estimates blew out to £18–24 billion (23–30bn USD) before the final project approval was deferred by the British government in mid-2016. While the initial plans were to have the first reactor running by the end of 2017 and grid-connected in 2018, construction was delayed as EDF pressured the UK government for guarantees and concessions that would 'allow an appropriate return on the massive investment required'. This support came in the form of a £10 billion government loan guarantee and a guaranteed 'strike price' of £92.50 MWh for thirty-five years, almost twice the current wholesale price – a difference that would be added to household energy bills.[16]

The UK National Audit Office has warned that the project could cost energy consumers £30 billion in top-up payments and the Department of Energy and Climate Change has recalculated the whole-of-life cost of the new reactors at £37 billion.[17] Negotiations also included unsubtle pressures to approve another new EDF project at Sizewell in Suffolk and CGN had also indicated its investment would be linked to the approval of a new reactor it would build at Bradwell, in Essex. That project had raised concerns about its impact on the ecologically sensitive Blackwater estuary, from which it would draw water for cooling.[18] The British government did not explain its July 2016 decision to defer approval, but the security services and UK Labour had raised concerns about a state-owned Chinese corporation building infrastructure crucial to the UK's energy security, especially given China's reputation for cyber espionage and its high-pressure tactics in the South China Sea.[19]

Other UK nuclear builds, such as Horizon Power's stations at Wylfa Anglesey and Oldbury in Gloucestershire, have been delayed after partners pulled out and there is widespread concern about the reluctance of private-sector investors to get involved in large nuclear projects.[20] Further complicating the nuclear lobby's narrative about climate change, the British government simultaneously cut small price subsidies for other renewable electricity generation options, such as wind and solar, causing bankruptcies in renewable firms.[21] Given that the nuclear industry has been so loudly proclaiming the value of nuclear power as a climate change solution, nothing could be more retrograde. Similar efforts to bargain the success of nuclear energy against renewables (rather than promote renewable and nuclear energy against fossil fuels) have occurred in Japan, with the Tokyo Electric Power Company (TEPCO) – the Fukushima plant's operator – opposing network pricing reforms in an effort to 'impede expansion of renewable energy capacity'.[22]

The Union of Concerned Scientists has estimated that the average cost of new nuclear power reactors is now $9 billion apiece and in 2009 published a report urging caution on the US Congress in committing taxpayer funds to subsidies for such projects. It pointed out planning failures in the US

nuclear industry in the 1960s and 1970s which saw electrical utilities abandoning some 100 plants during construction
and cost overruns for completed plants running to over
$200 billion. Taxpayers and electricity consumers paid some
$40 billion in extra costs due to the non-completed plants,
leading *Forbes* to call it 'the largest managerial disaster in
business history'. Citing the General Accounting Office's
advice that the risk of default on Department of Energy loan
guarantees is 50 per cent, they warn that the 'potential risk
exposure to the Federal government and taxpayers from guar-
anteeing nuclear loans could range from $360 billion (based
on 100 plants at today's projected cost) to $1.6 trillion (based
on 300 plants with costs 50% higher than today's estimates).'[23]
Wider-ranging studies show differential patterns globally,
with significant cost escalation in the USA and France and
much lower costs in later adopters of the technology such as
Japan, India, China and South Korea. Design standardization
and the co-location of reactors appears to suppress costs.[24]
There is also new research under way into much smaller
capacity reactors (50–300 MWe) which might enable the construction of plants with modular arrangements of reactors at
reduced cost and increased safety, due to their use of passive
cooling technology.[25]

Managing radioactive waste

A one gigawatt reactor produces approximately 21 tons of
highly radioactive fuel as waste per year; when multiplied
by the existing (and projected) number of working reactors,
this amounts to an environmental management problem
of great scale. Nuclear power stations produce 200,000 m^3
of low- and intermediate-level radioactive waste annually
and 10,000 m^3/12,000 tonnes of high-level waste including used reactor fuel.[26] The US government calculates that

68,000 tonnes of used nuclear fuel are stored at 72 commercial power plants and 2000 tonnes are added to that amount
every year.[27]

Radioactive wastes come in four forms, of which most
concerning are two: intermediate level wastes (ILW) which
contain high levels of radioactivity and require shielding
from the environment, but produce less heat than high-
level waste; and high-level wastes (HLW) produced by the
burning of uranium or mixed oxide fuel in a reactor, which
are highly radioactive and hot, requiring cooling and long-
term shielding from the environment. High-level waste
contains highly radioactive fission products such as cesium-
137 and strontium-90 (which produce ionizing radiation
with a strong ability to penetrate matter and have half-lives
of about thirty years) and a number of actinides including americium, neptunium, curium and several isotopes of
plutonium plus residual uranium-235. Plutonium-239 has
a half-life of 24,000 years; uranium-235 (which is also the
decay product of plutonium-239) has a half-life of 700 million years; and neptunium-237 has a half-life of two million
years. While the fission products are the most dangerous in
the early years of the waste's life, actinides and their daughter products dominate the radiotoxicity after 500 years and
thus create a long-term storage challenge. Plutonium can
also decay into soluble forms that can enter groundwater.[28]
High-level wastes are especially dangerous because they can
produce radiation doses that are fatal to humans and other
animals during even brief periods of direct exposure. As the
US Nuclear Regulatory Commission (NRC) explains, 'Ten
years after removal from a reactor, the surface dose rate from
a typical spent fuel assembly exceeds 10,000 rem/hour – far
greater than the fatal whole-body dose for humans of about
500 rem received all at once'.[29]

High-level waste from nuclear power plants is dealt with in

three ways, all of which ideally end in very long-term storage in a highly secure geological repository deep underground, which is sealed from aquifers and geologically stable. In the short term, spent fuel assemblies are stored for between three and ten years in pools on site, in order to provide radiation shielding and cool the waste. This is the case in all US nuclear power plants. (In Canada, regulators have ensured that fuel pools are housed in buildings remote from the reactors and following the Fukushima accident, plant operators have installed special devices to remove hydrogen from the air without power and installed portable generators and pumps that can operate after an accident.) After removal from the pools, spent fuel assemblies are put into reinforced casks of various designs, all of which must effectively shield the environment from the intense radiation within and are again stored on site. These designs include concrete canisters or silos and 'dry carbon' containers made of reinforced concrete and encased in shells made of carbon steel.[30]

In the UK, France, Japan, India and Russia, used fuel is 'reprocessed' to extract the usable plutonium and create mixed oxide (MOX) fuels that can be in turn used as new fuel assemblies in operating reactors. This process reduces the overall amount of waste to one fifth, but creates liquid HLW that must be solidified through vitrification into glass and placed into canisters. The IAEA estimates that some 5,550 tonnes of fuel is reprocessed annually (as of 2008) and out of a total historical global production of spent fuel of 268,000 tonnes in 2004, 90,000 tonnes (or 33%) had been reprocessed. Reprocessing is controversial. Separated plutonium is stored in powder form and is not highly radioactive and is thus vulnerable to theft. Given that less than twenty pounds of plutonium is required to build a simple nuclear device, the Union of Concerned Scientists estimated in 2009 that enough civil plutonium (some 250 tonnes) existed to build 30,000 nuclear weapons. The IAEA has admitted that 'large bulk handling facilities such as reprocessing plants are a challenge in terms of safeguards' against the diversion of fissile material to weapons uses that is prohibited by the NPT. In particular, even though such plants are subject to inspection there have been concerns about the statistical accuracy of measurements available to the IAEA and the potential for diversion. The United States has chosen not to approve reprocessing on non-proliferation grounds.[31]

Apart from the proliferation concerns around reprocessing (which the IAEA is trying to reduce), the licensing of plant operators to create, manage and transport nuclear waste is highly regulated around the world and subject to rigorous controls and inspections. This is backed up by numerous IAEA waste safety standards and conventions, including the Convention on the Physical Protection of Nuclear Material (1987) and the Joint Convention on the Safety of Spent Fuel Management and Other Radioactive Waste Management, which has 72 state members and entered into force in June 2001.[32] We can thus be confident that regulatory and technical solutions to radioactive waste storage are available and can be trusted under normal conditions. However the prospect of a terrorist attack on a nuclear facility with fuel pools, however unlikely, has raised concerns. The 9/11 Commission discovered that al-Qaeda had discussed crashing the planes into nuclear power plants and in 2004 the US Congress requested a study of the question from the National Academies of Sciences, Engineering and Medicine. Their report acknowledged that such an attack was a possibility and if it resulted in fuel assemblies being uncovered, could force evacuation of 3.5 million people and cost the US economy $700 billion. They said that better pool designs could mitigate the risk and that prompt transfer of fuel assemblies to dry cask storage after five years should be considered.

However the industry has resisted this action because of the additional costs involved.[33]

Over the longer term, secure storage in deep underground repositories is seen as the best option. However at the time of writing no such facilities had been opened, with the newest likely to open in Sweden in 2020. In 1987 the United States Congress designated Yucca Mountain in Nevada as the desired long-term storage site, which was supposed to begin accepting waste in 1998, but delays saw the US government being sued by power utilities with contracts at the site. Congressional opposition to the Nevada site suggests that it is likely to be abandoned and in 2010 President Obama created a commission to assess other disposal options. It recommended a 'phased, adaptive and consent-based approach' with the aim of having a geological repository available by 2048.[34] The Canadian Parliament established a Nuclear Waste Management Organization which recommended a similarly phased and consultative approach to identify a deep underground repository in the Canadian Shield. However this is not envisaged to be available for sixty years.[35] The French radioactive waste agency, Andra, is testing a site at Bure in northeast France, with hopes that it will be approved by the French National Assembly in 2016 and open in 2025. Sweden and Finland are also likely to approve sites between 2023 and 2025.[36] Australia, which produces a small amount of low and intermediate level waste, does not have near-term plans for a geological repository. However a Royal Commission appointed by the state government of South Australia has recommended that the government pursue long-term efforts to locate and open a geological waste facility that would take waste from around the world. They recommended that it be owned by the SA government and estimate that it could generate $51 billion in profits during its operation – which, if invested in a state wealth fund, could grow to $445 billion

over seventy years. They emphasized that political biparti-
sanship and stable government policy was essential and that
'local community consent is required . . . in the event that this
involves regional, remote and Aboriginal communities, consent processes must account for their particular values and
concerns.'[37]

In Australia, as in many other Western countries such as
Japan, Canada, the USA and Europe, there are strong anti-
nuclear sentiments, big environmental NGOs are normally
opposed to nuclear waste facilities and mines and the bitter
legacy that indigenous peoples have had with uranium has
only increased suspicions. Sweden and Finland appear to
have been careful to ensure that sites have been safe and
have engaged communities thoughtfully and sensitively,
often inviting them to volunteer to host facilities. Given the
long periods for which the waste must be stored and shielded
from the environment, considerable effort must be put into
ensuring that the sites are geologically stable for hundreds
of thousands of years and that technical storage solutions are
durable and trustworthy over the very long term.

The issues are complex. On the one hand, large uranium
exporters like Australia could be seen to have an ethical obli-
gation to provide long-term storage options, especially given
the enormous security and safety benefits of underground
storage (and relatively low risks) compared to current above-
ground solutions. The IAEA has emphasized that prolonging
interim above-ground waste storage creates risks and costs
that are better managed through deep geological disposal.[38]
Objections by environmentalists to underground depositories
fail to consider these security issues, the risks of which are
borne by the communities who live close to nuclear facilities. There are also major economic benefits to be gained by
hosting such facilities, especially if the profits are invested in
public goods. On the other hand, operators and governments

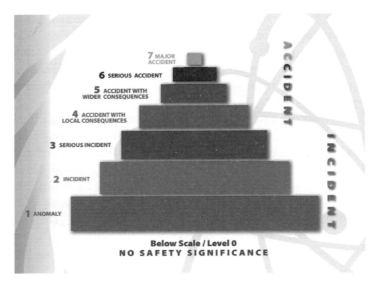

Level	Example
Below Scale/ Level 0	Slovenia, 2013
Level 1: anomaly	Finland, 2008
Level 2: incident	Paris, France, 2013
Level 3: serious incident	Lima, Peru, 2012
Level 4: accident with local consequences	New Delhi, India, 2010
Level 5: accident with wider consequences	Three Mile Island, USA, 1979
Level 6: serious accident	Kyshtym, Russian Federation, 1957
Level 7: major accident	Fukushima, Japan, 2011

Figure 5.1 The International Nuclear and Radiological Event Scale (INES)

Source: http://www-ns.iaea.org/downloads/iec/ines_flyer.pdf

must be transparent and committed to high levels of safety awareness, accountability and preparedness. Most importantly communities – especially indigenous communities – must be treated with consideration and their rights of veto respected. If governments are unwilling to be patient, consultative and transparent, it will be impossible to obtain community consent to these long-term storage solutions.

Nuclear safety and nuclear disaster

There have been over thirty serious accidents or incidents at nuclear plants since 1952 and more than seventy other incidents of a significant nature.[39] These are classified by the IAEA on a scale from 1 to 7 in severity – the International Nuclear and Radiological Events Scale (INES). Whereas a level 1 incident is termed an 'anomaly' and might involve the 'overexposure of a member of the public in excess of statutory annual limits', a level 7 incident is termed a 'major accident' and is defined as 'a major release of radioactive material with widespread health and environmental effects requiring implementation of planned and extended countermeasures'. Both the accidents at Chernobyl Ukraine in 1986 and Fukushima Japan in 2011 were classified as level 7 accidents. A level 6 incident is termed a 'serious accident' and involves a 'significant release of radioactive material'; a level 5 incident is termed 'an accident with wider consequences' that would involve 'a limited release of radioactive material' and 'several deaths from radiation'; and a level 4 'accident with local consequences' would involve 'a minor release of radioactive material' and 'at least one death from radiation'. Examples given of a level 4 incident include 'fuel melt or damage to fuel resulting in more than 0.1% release of core inventory' and 'the release of significant quantities of radioactive material within an installation with a high probability of significant exposure'. In short, every incident of 4 and above is extremely serious, involves mortality from radiation and – at levels 6 and 7 – high mortality and environmental consequences. Even a level 3 'serious incident' involves 'exposure in excess of ten times the statutory annual limit for workers' and would describe 'a nuclear accident . . . with no safety provisions remaining'.[40]

There have been eleven accidents INES-rated 4 and above, five rated 3 and the another five rated 2. One site, Sellafield in the UK (formerly known as Windscale), has had five separate incidents, the most recent in 2005. Some of the most severe accidents occurred early in the nuclear age in reactors or facilities used for weapons production (Windscale, Chalk River and Kyshtym), or in the case of Chernobyl power station, in an older Soviet reactor building design that was not considered safe by modern standards. However serious incidents have also occurred relatively recently, including at Sellafield, Fukushima and Onagawa (2011), Fleurus in Belgium (2006, level 4) and Forsmark Sweden (2006, level 2).[41]

Prior to Chernobyl and Fukushima, the most serious nuclear power station accident was at Three Mile Island near Harrisburg Pennsylvania in 1979 (level 5), in a 1000 MW pressurized water reactor. In a typical nuclear accident scenario, cooling of the reactor core failed when feedwater pumps stopped and heat and pressure increased even as control rods were inserted to terminate the chain reaction. A stuck safety valve and a series of interpretation errors by the human reactor operators deprived the reactor of coolant which caused partial meltdown of the nuclear fuel, the venting of radioactive material into the atmosphere and 700,000 gallons of radioactive water flooding the reactor building. A dangerous 'pressure pulse' of radioactive hydrogen from the reactor core also escaped, but was not strong enough to burst the containment dome. Hence only small amounts of radioactivity were released to the surrounding environment. George Charpak and Richard Garwin explain that 'the formation of a hydrogen bubble had not been seen in any of the accident scenarios imagined by governmental regulatory authorities' and assert that 'good luck as much as skill averted the evolution of the 1979 Three Mile Island accident into a catastrophe'.[42]

Chernobyl and Fukushima
The accidents at Chernobyl and Fukushima were the result of a combination of both design flaws and human error and – especially in Japan – their resultant effects were compounded by poor post-event decision-making and disaster management policies. In the case of Fukushima, the vulnerability of the facility to a tsunami was compounded by an insular culture within Japan's nuclear industry and regulatory community which clung to a 'myth of 100% safety'.

The Chernobyl plant is located 130 km north of Kiev and 70 km south of Ukraine's border with Belarus. Three km from the reactor was a purpose-built city, Pripyat, housing 50,000 people and 15 km away the old town of Chernobyl with a population of 12,000. It had four 1,000 MW reactors of the Soviet RBMK–1,000 design, which had two major flaws that distinguish them from more modern Western designs. They used graphite rather than water as a neutron moderator to stimulate fission, which meant that under low power conditions they could create what is called 'a positive void coefficient' in which the steam produced *increases* the reactivity and 'the reactor becomes unstable and prone to sudden power surges'.[43] Other pressurized or boiling light water reactor designs use water as a moderator as well as a coolant, which produces a negative void coefficient and increases safety. The other major flaw was a lack of a reinforced concrete containment structure (of the kind that averted catastrophe at Three Mile Island) surrounding the reactor core and high-pressure piping.

The accident took place on 26 April 1986 during a planned

shutdown for maintenance of the Unit 4 reactor, when staff decided to take the opportunity to test 'whether, in the event of a loss of station power, the slowing turbine could provide enough electrical power to operate the emergency equipment in the core cooling water circulating pumps until the diesel emergency power supply became operative'. Prior to the test, the emergency core cooling system was disabled while control rods were inserted to reduce power. An operational error then saw power fall to a very low level and a positive void coefficient come into play, causing reactor power levels to become very unstable. Then operators reduced the flow of cooling feed water, exaggerating the instability and a massive power surge occurred which ruptured the fuel core and caused two explosions that destroyed the reactor. A plume of smoke, highly radioactive fission products and burning debris from the destroyed reactor core rose a kilometre into the atmosphere and was blown to the northwest of the plant. A number of fires broke out on site and were extinguished within four hours after enormous bravery by firefighters, thirty-one of whom were exposed to lethal doses of radiation and subsequently died. However a fire then broke out in the highly radioactive graphite moderator material in the destroyed core, which was exposed to the atmosphere and burned for eleven days.[44]

This long-lived radioactive plume deposited iodine-131, cesium-134 and cesium-137 (with half-lives respectively of eight days, two years and thirty years) in 'a complex and variable exposure pattern' most intensely across Belarus, Ukraine and Russia, but also further into Europe. Iodine-131 was a major immediate concern because of its take-up in the thyroid gland and its likelihood of causing cancer. This is especially dangerous to children, who have a comparatively larger thyroid and consume contaminated milk products; the incidence of thyroid cancer among children in these regions rose sharply in the years following the accident, with more than

6000 childhood thyroid cancer cases diagnosed by 2005.[45]
134 Chernobyl workers received high doses and suffered radiation sickness and twenty-eight died in the first three months;
another 530,000 registered recovery operation workers also
received substantial doses between 1986 and 1990, a cohort
that is still 'at potential risk of late consequences such as
cancer and other diseases'. Another not inconsiderable health
impact resulted from the anxiety of communities affected by
fear, dislocation and loss of livelihood. Health studies do not
predict any measurable effects in Europe outside these three
countries, although Scandinavia was more strongly affected
by elevated exposures to radiation.[46]

135,000 people were evacuated permanently from the towns
of Pripyat and Chernobyl and other villages and farms within a
30 km radius of the plant, although by 1999 more than 8,000
people were still living in areas subject to evacuation.[47] The
economic impact and cost of the accident have been enormous,
estimated at 'over two decades, hundreds of billions of dollars',
related to the costs of managing and sealing of the site, the
resettlement of people, social protection and health care, radiation monitoring of the environment, the disposal of radioactive
waste and soil and the opportunity cost of removing agricultural land (some 784,327 ha) and forests from use including
the closure of agricultural and industrial facilities. Between 5
and 7 per cent of Ukraine's government budget was devoted to
Chernobyl-related programmes and 22.3 per cent of Belarus'
national budget was also devoted to such programmes in 1991,
declining to 6.1 per cent in 2002. Total spending by Belarus
between 1991 and 2003 was estimated at over US$13 billion.
Localized economic recession hit the radiation-affected areas,
depressing wages and increasing unemployment and the
impact was compounded by the collapse of the Soviet Union
and the Russian economic crisis of 1998.[48]

The Fukushima Daiichi power plant is operated by the

Tokyo Electric Power Company (TEPCO), on the east coast of the Japanese island of Honshu, some 200 km north of Tokyo and a few kilometres southeast of the town of Fukushima. Built on the site of a former Pacific War air base, the complex comprises six boiling water reactors (BWR) designed by General Electric. At the time of the accident Units 1, 2 and 3 of the plant were running, but Units 4, 5 and 6 were in cold shutdown for servicing. The fuel in reactor 4 had been transferred to a storage pool located at the high level of its reactor building; one of the distinctive design features of the Fukushima reactors were storage pools for highly radioactive spent fuel built high on one side of the building 'in a very exposed position'. Unit 3 had also been fuelled with a batch of mixed oxide (MOX) fuel containing about 230 kg of plutonium-239.[49]

Like other major accidents, such as Chernobyl and Three Mile Island, the issue was a loss of coolant water to control the enormous temperatures the reactor fuel was capable of reaching. The crisis was triggered on 11 March 2011 when a massive earthquake – later confirmed to have been at level 9 on the Richter scale – occurred with its epicentre in the Pacific Ocean seabed 66 km east of Sendai (which is less than 90 km north of the plant). The quake was so powerful that it rattled the ionosphere, disrupted navigational signals, shifted the island of Honshu 2.4 metres eastwards and triggered two massive tsunamis that surged towards the Japanese coast at 600 km/h. When the tsunamis crossed the coastline south of the power station they were recorded at 21 metres (70 feet) in height; some 10 billion tonnes of water smashed into the northern Honshu coast, overwhelming concrete defences and destroying entire towns, farms and factories as much as 10 km inland and flooding an area more than 500 km^2. The tsunami killed some 15,891 people and over 2500 remained missing as of April 2015.[50]

Three other nuclear plants were also hit by the tsunami:

Fukushima Daini, 12 km to the south (operated by TEPCO); Onagawa, 116 km north (operated by Tohoku Electric Power); and Tokai Daini, 112 km south (operated by the Japan Atomic Power Company). Onagawa was closer to the earthquake's epicentre than Fukushima Daiichi, but the plant was elevated to 15 metres with a 14 metre seawall and was largely spared from severe inundation. It also lost all but one of its external power lines and two of its three backup generators and had a fire in one of its turbine buildings. The crisis was classed as a level 1 on the INES scale. At Daini, which was classified as a level 3 accident, the tsunami was largely held back by the seawall and flooding was limited. The plant lost three of four seawater pumps and nine of twelve emergency generators, but one of the off-site power lines remained intact and workers were able to connect cables to this last remaining power source to operate the cooling systems for three of the four reactors in danger of melting down.[51]

When the earthquake hit, the operating reactors at Fukushima Daiichi were scrammed automatically and control rods introduced to halt the chain reactions under way; however the reactor cores still generate large amounts of heat even when non-critical.[52] The earthquake had felled transmission lines and wrecked electrical substations, cutting power to the plant, which triggered emergency diesel generators. At this time, even though the vibrations had exceeded the plant's design standards, cooling systems were still working. However the tsunami, which reached 15 metres at the site, flooded all but one of the diesel generators, cut all power to Units 1, 2, 3 and 4 and damaged surrounding roads which made access later difficult. This left all three operating reactors in a very dangerous situation: within four hours, water had dropped below the level of the fuel rods in Unit 1 and meltdown had begun. Over the next four days all three reactors melted down and intense hydrogen explosions ruptured the containments, venting radioactivity into the atmosphere. (Hydrogen is created when the protective zirconium cladding around the uranium fuel reacts with steam at high temperatures.) The spent fuel pools were also a major concern: the pool in Unit 4 had been manufactured without the required bracing and was damaged in the earthquake, releasing coolant and breaking fuel rods. Concerted efforts were made over the next days and months to ensure that the fuel remained covered and to remove fuel assemblies.[53] If the fuel pools had failed and burned through their floors they would have released extraordinary amounts of radiation and required an evacuation radius of up to 300 km.[54] In relation to this scenario, the independent investigation commission has commented that 'it would have required planned evacuations of some thirty million people from the Tokyo region'.[55] The explosions spread radiation – in the form of iodine-131, cesium-134 and 137, plutonium-239 and strontium-90 – around the plant and northwest in a large plume towards Fukushima city. The central part of the plume saw levels of three million becquerels (Bq) of cesium per square metre measured, a zone outside it with 1–3 million Bq and a further outer zone with 0.6–1 million Bq. Radiation was also spread into the ocean from the release of contaminated water. The total radiation released into the environment is believed to have been one tenth of the amount released by Chernobyl and forced widespread evacuations and controls over food and fish distribution and sale.[56]

The disaster uncovered multiple failures of plant design and safety, emergency response and coordination and regulatory oversight. In terms of prevention, the company had not considered seriously enough the combination of an earthquake *and* tsunami cutting power and overwhelming backup systems. The Fukushima plant was protected by a 5.7 m sea wall, but TEPCO and Japanese regulators ignored new and compelling evidence about the risk of tsunamis overwhelming existing defences: 'in 1993 NISA [The Nuclear and Industrial Safety Agency] called on utilities to develop backup power systems in order to prevent a station blackout in the event of a tsunami, but the utilities lobbied regulators and did not institute such measures'. In 2009 TEPCO and the regulator had also discussed the implications of new simulations and archaeological evidence that a 9.2 metre tsunami could occur, but the power company decided that a higher sea wall was prohibitively expensive. Its own engineers had made similar warnings in 2008. Even worse, a highly critical TEPCO internal enquiry conducted after the disaster admitted that 'some suggested safety improvements, such as using multiple power sources and cooling systems, would require the plant's temporary closure and add to its costs'. The TEPCO report revealed that managers feared that 'if the company were to implement a severe accident response plan, it would spur anxiety throughout the country and in the communities where nuclear plants are sited and lend momentum to the antinuclear movement'. The report stated that 'the company should have adhered more closely to international safety standards for atomic facilities and trained specialist staff and practical disaster response, rather than relying on safety drills it dismissed as a "formality"'. The ministry had shut down all of TEPCO's reactors in 2002 because media reports had revealed that the government had failed to act on information about the 'systematic falsification of repair and maintenance records' by the company. As Jeff Kingston concluded, 'This unjustified insouciance and penurious approach cost Japan dearly; TEPCO's bottom line mattered more than public safety.'[57]

The government and company response was also problematic. The earthquake had destroyed the operations centre at the plant and luckily staff could evacuate to a newly constructed emergency operations centre built on higher ground and resistant to earthquakes that had been completed just eight months before. 'Had this structure not existed,' remarked one commentator, 'the lack of a viable on-site staging ground rescue operation would likely lead to a significantly worse outcome'. On the third night of the crisis, the TEPCO president was apparently considering asking the Prime Minister if he would permit the company to abandon the site entirely. Prime Minister Kan instead ordered a joint government-TEPCO headquarters established within TEPCO to coordinate the operations.[58] There were failures to transmit information between the stricken plant, TEPCO headquarters, NISA, the Nuclear Safety Commission and the Japanese government and the concealment from the public of key information.[59]

On 11 March the government established a compulsory evacuation and exclusion zone of 3 km around the plant then expanded it to 10 km the next day and asked people within 30 km to stay indoors. Ten days later, on 25 March, it recommended voluntary evacuation from within the 30 km zone. On 25 April the government made evacuation compulsory from within 30 km of the plant and the zone between 30 and 40 km was declared a voluntary evacuation zone. Eventually 154,000 people would be evacuated, the majority of whom cannot return to their homes. TEPCO workers were joined by a skilled 'veterans corps' of over 160 retired engineers who entered the damaged reactor buildings to carry out repairs and manage the crisis, wearing radiation-resistant suits and working in ten-minute shifts. Seven months after the tsunami three of the volunteers had died, one of a heart attack, another of an acute form of leukemia and a third of undisclosed causes. They were joined by some 18,000 poorly paid day-labourers who worked on site and were issued with dosimeters to ensure that their radiation exposure remain within a raised level set by the Ministry of Health of 250 millisieverts (mSv) per year (increased from the pre-crisis level of

20 mSv per year). Richard Broinowski has commented that 'this new level "legalized" illnesses and deaths from radiation exposure at the reactors, or at least absolved the government or TEPCO of responsibility for them . . . cumulative doses of radiation were not recorded and therefore cancers they may later develop cannot with any certitude be legally attributed'.[60]

The United Nations Scientific Committee on the Effects of Atomic Radiation (UNSCEAR) issued a 2013 report and a follow-up study which predicted that 'an increased risk of cancer would be expected' for 160 workers who received effective doses over 100 mSv and that twelve workers who received increased doses of iodine-131 had an increased risk of developing thyroid cancer. For adults in Fukushima prefecture it estimated 'average lifetime effective doses to be of the order of 10 mSv or less and first-year doses to be one-third to one-half of that'. They commented that 'risk models by inference suggest increased cancer risk', but that cancers induced by radiation are difficult to distinguish from other causes. In general and especially in relation to Chernobyl, they state that doses to the general public 'are generally low or very low' and that the most important health effect is 'on mental and social well-being, related to the enormous impact of the earthquake, tsunami and nuclear accident and the fear and stigma related to the perceived risk of exposure to ionizing radiation'.[61] Nineteen hospital patients died after being left for five days with limited food and medical supplies during the mishandled evacuation of Futaba hospital. A total of 1867 people have died from stress-related illnesses and other maladies (including suicide and PTSD) in the Fukushima prefecture after the triple disaster – over and above the 1607 people who died during the tsunami and earthquake. In March 2014 136,000 people remained displaced from their homes and towns and a year later the number was 120,000. The Japan Times has published annual editorials on the anniversary of the tsunami highly critical of what they perceived to be 'denial' in the health ministry, saying that government should be giving more medical, social and housing support to displaced communities.[62]

An important study of Japan's triple disaster places emphasis on its broad-based and very negative impacts on *human security* in Japan. This supports the arguments of Chapter 3 – which asked critical questions about whether nuclear weapons support or undermine global security – this time asking the same questions of the ways in which modern societies manage the risks involved in nuclear power. It is estimated that the Fukushima disaster alone will cost ¥11.08 trillion ($105 billion) including compensation to residents, radiation cleanup and storage of soil, and costs involved in dismantling the stricken plant. Other estimates suggest that $100 billion will be required to decommission the plant and that the total cost will reach some $400 billion, much of which will be paid by the Japanese government or added to energy bills.[63]

Risk and consequences
The World Nuclear Association insists that 'nuclear power is a safe means of generating electricity' and that 'the risk of accidents in nuclear power plants is low and declining'. They assert that Three Mile Island, Chernobyl and Fukushima are 'the only major accidents to have occurred in over 16,000 cumulative reactor years of commercial nuclear power operation in thirty-three countries ... the consequences of an accidental terrorist attack are minimal compared with other commonly accepted risks. Radiological effects on people of any radioactive releases can be avoided.'[64] This may be true, but must be considered against a countervailing truism: that when one considers the dramatic environmental, social and economic impacts of a major nuclear accident, as demonstrated by the aftermath of Fukushima, nuclear accidents are paradigmatic cases of low probability but high consequence

events. Nuclear fuel stored onsite is arguably a major risk when one considers the possibility of terrorism; nuclear plants contain enormous physical forces and complex interfaces of machine and human processes that can combine unpredictably in a crisis; and ageing plant must be carefully monitored, key components replaced and timely decisions to retire reactors must be undertaken. The dramatic failures in safety and regulatory independence and oversight exposed after Fukushima – in a country extraordinarily vulnerable to seismic disturbance – were especially concerning. It exposed how reluctant management was, when protected by a cosy relationship with government, to address new and evolving information about risk and invest in enhanced protections. This ensured that lower probabilities would become higher probabilities with higher consequences. It raises a significant question of whether national governments can be trusted to regulate nuclear safety entirely alone and whether enhanced international machinery is worth considering.

Regulating the nuclear industry

The civilian-led Independent Investigation Commission on the Fukushima Nuclear Accident argued that a major human and societal factor in the disaster was 'the "myth of safety", which is said to have been constructed to win over the local populations near the sites of nuclear plants'. Citing numerous testimonies by officials, it said that a culture emerged 'within which it was taboo to suggest that safety could ever be further improved'. In particular, they singled out the Nuclear Safety Commission's belief that 'the total loss of AC power for an extended length of time was the contingency that need not be contemplated'.[65] They also cited a former high-level official at METI who admitted that 'NISA can neither stand up to TEPCO nor properly act as its regulator'. Critics speak of the existence of 'a full-scale [nuclear] "village" – a giant, interwoven, interdependent community' that draws in political parties and media dependent on donations and advertising, labour unions, researchers and former government officials who 'pass through a revolving door into electric power companies' according to the system of *amakudari*. Fukushima plant workers had told of 'being routinely warned in advance of inspections and inspectors did not seem eager to uncover violations'.[66]

In September 2012 the Japanese government and Diet created a single agency to regulate the nuclear power industry, replacing the Nuclear Safety Commission and NISA with the Nuclear Regulation Authority (NRA). Whereas the previous agencies reported to the Ministry of Economy, Trade and Industry (METI), which had a mandate to promote nuclear energy, the NRA exists as an external agency of the Ministry of the Environment and its leadership is appointed by the Diet.[67] However questions have been raised about the decision-making of the NRA, especially its approval of life-extensions for reactors over forty years of age. The meltdowns at Fukushima took place in reactors commissioned between thirty-five and forty years before; given that three of Japan's reactors are over forty years old and another sixteen are over thirty years old, concerns about metal fatigue and dated technology are salient. A new law requires the decommissioning of ageing plants after forty years, but also creates a loophole that will permit operation beyond that at the discretion of regulators. This has occurred in Fukui prefecture where the NRA approved a twenty-year extension of operation for the Mihama No. 3 reactor and also for Takahama Nos. 1 and 2, both of which are operated by Kansai Electric Power. Mihama is close to a tectonic fault and the reactor will require expensive safety upgrades and it is likely that local residents will challenge the approval in court.[68] There have also been large street demonstrations in central Tokyo and opinion polling shows that many Japanese oppose the restarting of mothballed reactors.[69]

Fukushima and its aftermath demonstrate the fragmenting levels of trust in national-level regulatory and oversight regimes for nuclear safety. Yet, as a 2011 International Institute for Strategic Studies analysis states, 'there is no [international] safety verification mechanism akin to the IAEA non-proliferation safeguards regime' and we are instead reliant upon 'a complex web of international conventions, organizations and best-practice guidance [that] seeks to harmonize and improve safety arrangements'. After 2011 the IAEA began actively promoting the 1994 international Convention on Nuclear Safety (which currently has 78 state members, with 10 signatories not having yet ratified) as a voluntary mechanism that aims to 'legally commit participating States operating land-based nuclear power plants to maintain a high level of safety by setting international benchmarks' – these benchmarks are set out in the IAEA Safety Fundamentals document 'Fundamental Safety Principles (SF-1)'.[70] At a February 2015 meeting of the contracting parties to the convention, members directly noted the Fukushima Daiichi accident and called on 'all national regulators to identify provisions to prevent and mitigate the potential for severe accidents with off-site consequences'. There they adopted the Vienna Declaration on Nuclear Safety, which set out three principles to prevent accidents. Briefly, the principles insisted that: any new nuclear power plants must be designed, sited and constructed with the objective of preventing accidents and mitigating releases of radionuclides; comprehensive and systematic safety assessments must be carried out regularly on existing installations throughout their lifetime; and national requirements and regulations must take into account relevant IAEA safety standards.[71]

The IAEA has been highly active in attempting to formulate rigorous safety standards and have them adopted by member states with nuclear power, most recently sending its Integrated Regulatory Review Service (IRRS) team to Kenya to assess its regulatory framework on radiation safety and signing new agreements with Russia to strengthen coordination of the application of radiation safety and monitoring programmes.[72] While the commitment of the IAEA to strengthening nuclear safety internationally cannot be questioned, the Convention on Nuclear Safety still provides states with the responsibility and freedom to create their own nuclear safety regimes and merely requires member states to 'submit reports on the implementation of their obligations for "peer review" at meetings of the parties to be held at the IAEA'.[73] Each national report is reviewed by a group of member states and the IAEA is able to also make a 'report presenting observations on significant issues related to the safety of nuclear installations' based on all information available to it since the last meeting.[74] While such a process of dialogue and transparency through peer pressure is certainly valuable, this regime lacks the force and universality of the Additional Protocol to the NPT which aims to prevent the diversion of fissile material to weapons programmes. Implementing the standards set out in the Convention requires a comprehensive integration of national planning controls, management commitment, safety measures and regulatory independence – a system with multiple potential points of failure. If a national government or regulator were to egregiously fail to implement these standards there is little that the IAEA or CNS membership could do. The Japanese experience arguably demonstrates the need for a much stronger, mandatory international framework – one that gives the IAEA more resources and powers to make inspections and issue binding orders to governments and power plant operators.

Conclusion: an uncertain future

The Fukushima disaster cast (an at least temporary) chill over the nuclear industry's grand expansionary plans as political leaders responded to community concerns over safety. All of Japan's fifty-four operating reactors, which supplied a third of Japan's power, were shut down while stress tests were undertaken. Japan's Prime Minister Yoshihiko Noda stated he would like to phase out nuclear power over the next few decades, a view reflected in an October 2011 white paper on nuclear power, but as discussed above, restarts have begun against a background of considerable community anxiety. Germany, Italy, Belgium and Switzerland also resolved to phase out nuclear power over the next few decades and Europe's largest electrical engineering company, Siemens, announced it was withdrawing from the nuclear industry and would end its collaboration with Russia's Rosatom in the construction of new nuclear plants.[75]

The nuclear industry responded robustly to these developments: the World Energy Council stated that there is no sign of decreased demand from outside the countries listed above and the Director-General of the World Nuclear Association charged that 'countries like Germany will soon demonstrate the economic and environmental irresponsibility of allowing politicians to set important national policies in the middle of a panic attack . . . many national leaders who soberly reviewed their energy strategies have reaffirmed the conclusion they reached before Fukushima: that nuclear power is a uniquely reliable and expandable source of low-carbon energy that can be safely used to meet clean-energy need'.[76] Some growth in nuclear power capacity, especially in India and China, is likely and a large number of existing reactors will continue to operate to and possibly beyond their projected lifetimes. However, between the tremendous financing challenges of new nuclear power stations, the toxic climate change debate and government mismanagement of low carbon energy strategies in many Western states and community suspicion of nuclear energy, there are questions about whether aging plants will be replaced by new nuclear reactors or less complex solar, wind and tidal technologies. Addressing the range of very salient concerns about safety has thus become crucial, both for protecting the human security of communities around nuclear power plants and for the strategic future of the industry. It may not survive another Fukushima.

CHAPTER SIX

Challenges and Futures

Every five years, the 189 state members of the NPT hold a 'review conference' ('Revcon') in New York City at the headquarters of the United Nations. Delegates fill the General Assembly, foreign ministers and celebrities give speeches, NGOs and researchers give seminars and press conferences and teams of diplomats negotiate for a month over a long text that sets out a report card on the state of global disarmament and non-proliferation, sets out future directions and is meant to be adopted by consensus. The last meeting, held throughout the month of May in 2015, was the ninth such conference. Millions of dollars were spent on security, accommodation, food and limousines, yet the conference failed to agree an outcome. This embarrassing stalemate was a palpable demonstration of the deep divisions and fissures in the nuclear non-proliferation regime. The ostensible deadlock was Israel's objection to a rigid Egyptian proposal for a conference on a Middle East zone free of weapons of mass destruction, which broke with a fragile consensus about the issue and brought about the ironic situation in which the United States, Britain and Canada blocked a major international treaty review on behalf of a state that is not even a member of the treaty. However this was just one point of contention. The meeting highlighted a series of major fractures in the regime around the pace of disarmament, efforts to strengthen non-proliferation through the control of fissile materials and the nuclear fuel cycle and whether the NPT itself is adequate or needs to be supplemented by new legal arrangements such as a treaty that would ban nuclear weapons *as such*.[1]

The regime had already been shaken by North Korea's nuclear tests and its withdrawal from the Treaty and by revelations that Iran was seeking to enrich uranium well beyond what was needed for peaceful uses and may well have been planning to develop a nuclear weapon. This exposed what has been termed the 'Article X problem', in which states could use the right to peaceful uses embodied in the NPT to develop nuclear weapons in secret and then withdraw from the treaty with impunity.[2] Strategic and political tensions between the USA and Russia were growing, given the sanctions imposed after Russia's intervention in Ukraine, mutual accusations that the other side had violated the 1987 Intermediate-Range Nuclear Forces Treaty and ongoing disputes about ballistic missile defence (BMD) and NATO expansion. Relations between China and the United States were also cooling, amid news that China was introducing MIRVed warheads on some of its missiles, apparently in an effort to maintain deterrence in the face of advances in American BMD research.[3] Meanwhile the USA and Russia were engaging in expensive weapons modernization programmes even as they implemented the weapons reductions under the New START treaty.

UN Secretary-General Ban Ki-Moon summed up this disturbing picture in an address to the first day of the conference:

> ... recent developments indicate that the trend towards nuclear zero is reversing. Instead of progress towards new arms reduction agreements, we have allegations about destabilizing violations of existing agreements. Instead of a Comprehensive Nuclear Test-Ban Treaty in force or a treaty banning the production of fissile materials for nuclear weapons, we see expensive modernization programmes that will entrench nuclear weapons for decades to come. Instead

of pursuing proposals to accelerate nuclear disarmament . . . there has been a dangerous return to Cold War mentalities. This reversal is a regression for our world.[4]

Ban Ki-Moon saw more hope in the Joint Comprehensive Plan of Action (JCPOA) that would be signed six weeks later and provide a framework to restrain Iran's enrichment programme for fifteen years; but it came after numerous military threats and the imposition of harsh sanctions which halved Iran's oil exports and plunged its economy into a deep recession.[5] It was a coerced solution rather than one which genuinely resolved the fears and problems that produced it.

Out of this situation of stalemate and uncertainty, this chapter looks ahead. It considers what futures lie ahead for the nuclear non-proliferation regime and its attempt to construct a global nuclear order that can prevent the spread and the use of nuclear weapons and eventually see their abolition. Will it survive and in what form? How might it better evolve? And what other nuclear legacies does the international community need to be addressing? As well as the bitterness between miners and indigenous communities discussed in Chapter 4, which will lock away vast reserves of the mineral for decades to come, the Cold War weapons complex also left an ongoing legacy of waste and contamination. Sites such as Sellafield (UK), Hanford (USA) and Mayak (Russia) store thousands of tonnes of nuclear waste, some of which has been deliberately dumped into nearby seas, rivers and groundwater. Cleanup efforts costing tens of billions of dollars have been mismanaged and remain unfinished.[6]

In Chapter 1, this book spoke of how uranium is a profoundly materially active substance – an 'actant' – which gave rise to complex moral, political and strategic questions about how it should be exploited, how it would transform human societies and the system of international relations and how its

Table 6.1 Global Nuclear Warheads 2015 (Updated October 2015)				
	Stockpiled	Deployed	Retired	Total
United States	4,717	1,538	2,340	7,100
Russia	4,500	1,658	3,200	7,700
France	300			300
China	260			260
United Kingdom	225			225
Pakistan	120			120
India	120			120
Israel	80			80
DPRK	8			8
				15,913

Source: Arms Control Association http://www.armscontrol.org/factsheets/ Nuclearweaponswhohaswhat (accessed on 6 January 2016)

innate properties and dangers would trouble every attempt to bring it under rational use and control. Many decades after the complex pattern of decisions which decided many of these questions, we are left with the historical costs of the nuclear industry and enormous short- and long-term challenges, some extending for thousands of years. One of the most profound and immediate of those challenges is disarmament.

NPT futures

As this book was being completed, there were some 15,500 nuclear weapons on earth possessed by nine states, with approximately 10,000 in military service and the rest awaiting dismantlement. The majority are held by the United States and Russia, with 7,100 and 7,700 respectively. As of March 2016, the USA had deployed 1,735 strategic warheads on 521 ICBMs, SLBMs and strategic bombers and Russia had

1,481 strategic nuclear warheads deployed on 741 ICBMs, SLBMs and strategic bombers.[7] They also possess thousands of non-strategic (or tactical) warheads of varying yields which are not subject to any arms control measures. Each of them, especially the strategic weapons, possess enormous potential for destruction, toxicity and loss of life and even a small nuclear exchange in which between fifty and one hundred weapons were used could trigger a new Ice Age and devastate global food security. These are the raw material facts that the member states of the NPT now confront.

The global nuclear order has three potential futures: it can muddle through with the same number of nuclear states and nuclear weapons and hope that nuclear weapons are not used by states or terrorists; it could break apart and new states acquire nuclear weapons and withdraw from the NPT or existing states abandon arms-control and revert to Cold War postures; or, if infused with a new collective sense of the common danger and responsibility, it could transition to 'zero', a world with few or no nuclear weapons. The current situation is pregnant with all three possibilities, but events are likely to converge on one of two paths: unchecked proliferation and the unravelling of the NPT, or a strengthening of international architectures towards abolition. Like the uranium atom itself, the current situation is inherently fissile and unstable and cannot be trusted to hold. Not only is the strategic environment too unpredictable, but political divides within the NPT are now intensifying as a key group of states increases pressure on disarmament and seeks to remind the world of the ethical and humanitarian implications of nuclear weapons. My view is that unless the world actively moves towards abolition in a way that promotes strategic stability, the outcome will be the destruction of the NPT regime and a very dangerous and unpredictable future.

Two key problems in the nuclear order have emerged over the last few decades and now threaten to unravel it. They relate to the ways in which key groups of states interpret the fundamental 'bargain' at the heart of the NPT regime – that which exchanges active efforts towards nuclear disarmament and abolition on the part of the nuclear weapons states for an observance of non-proliferation rules by the rest. This bargain is arguably now under extreme stress.

On disarmament, the nuclear weapon states had negotiated wording prior to the Treaty's adoption that relieved them of having to agree to a clear timetable for disarmament. Now, even after numerous NPT review conferences have seen an overwhelmingly strong consensus that nuclear abolition must be the end-state and that progress must accelerate, it is clear that some nuclear weapons states (or significant political constituencies within them) do not believe in disarmament as a process of abolition at all. Whereas many states have engaged in arms-control or limited reductions (and publicly portray them as showing their commitment to disarmament), they appear to see nuclear abolition as, at best, a very long-term goal. Russia is modernizing its nuclear capability and is uninterested in talks with the United States over a follow-up treaty to New START; the Obama administration has offered to resume negotiations but has also announced a plan to modernize the existing capability, while major sections of the Republican Party and Congress opposed the New START treaty and show complete disdain for the United States' obligations under the NPT. France has eliminated its land-based missiles and announced a ceiling of three hundred warheads as a deterrent of 'strict sufficiency', but President François Hollande stated just a few weeks before the 2015 Revcon that nuclear abolition remains a 'long-term goal, when the strategic context allows'.[8]

The United Kingdom has reduced its stockpile to 225 warheads, with 120 operational and only forty deployed on one submarine at any time, but also has shown no indications of being committed to abolition. In July 2016 the British Parliament voted for the renewal of the 'Trident' SLBM system, which will involve spending up to £40 billion on new submarines and other infrastructure. Yet the Scottish National Party opposed the renewal of Trident, the Liberal Democrats advocate a 'step down the nuclear ladder', and there are strong divisions within the British Labour Party over the issue.[9] A particularly unhelpful element has been the politicization of the UK debate, with Conservative Party leaders calling the Labour leader Jeremy Corbyn a 'threat to national security' and saying in Parliament that 'some members of the Labour Party seem to be the first to defend the country's enemies'.[10] China, which maintains a triad of forces with 160 deployed weapons, expresses verbal support for disarmament, but has made no effective gestures itself. India and Pakistan maintain a distrustful bilateral relationship and are engaged in modernizing their nuclear capabilities.[11] Meanwhile Israel continues to refuse to either confirm its possession of nuclear weapons or join the NPT and actively resists international pressure to engage on the issue, as the 2015 Revcon outcome demonstrated. Its internal political climate suggests that an open discussion and a subsequent movement towards disarmament could not occur any time soon.

At the 2000 NPT review conference, and again in 2010, the nuclear weapons states committed to 'accelerate concrete progress on the steps leading to nuclear disarmament' including 'rapidly moving towards an overall reduction in the global stockpile of all types of nuclear weapons' and to 'discuss policies that prevent the use of nuclear weapons and eventually lead to their elimination'. They also committed to reduce the risk of accidental use, to enhance transparency and 'diminish the role and significance of nuclear weapons in all military and security concepts, doctrines and policies'.[12] However, as one influential study of global progress against the commitments set out in the 2010 review conference outcome concluded, the nuclear weapon states had made no or minimal progress towards these goals in the fifteen years since they were laid out in 2000.[13]

The three state-sponsored international conferences on the humanitarian implications of nuclear war, followed by the humanitarian pledge and General Assembly resolution, were a direct outcome of the non-nuclear weapons states' frustration at the stalemate on disarmament and the determination by the nuclear weapon states to frustrate multi-lateral negotiations in the Conference On Disarmament.[14] This frustration only increased with the failure of the 2015 review conference and the much weaker language on disarmament in (leaked) drafts of the outcome than was contained in the 2010 official outcome and action plan.[15] We should recall the very strong language in the humanitarian pledge adopted by the General Assembly with the affirmative votes of 139 governments. It calls on 'all stakeholders, States, international organizations, the International Red Cross and Red Crescent Movement, parliamentarians and civil society' to 'cooperate in efforts to stigmatize, prohibit and eliminate nuclear weapons in the light of their unacceptable humanitarian consequences and associated risks'.[16]

As a result the non-nuclear weapons states have taken an important step that seizes the agenda from the nuclear weapon states and may go a long way to breaking the deadlock. They have revived the Open-Ended Working Group On Taking Forward Multi-lateral Nuclear Disarmament Negotiations (OEWG), which was re-established with a General Assembly resolution 70/33 of 7 December 2015. It has two main aims. Firstly, to 'substantively address *concrete effective legal measures, legal provisions and norms* that would need to be concluded to attain and maintain a world without nuclear weapons'.[17] This incorporates a number of ideas – from a simple nuclear weapons prohibition treaty to a full-scale Nuclear Weapons Convention that would underpin a fully disarmed world – and aims at accelerating progress on negotiating the text of such a document without the nuclear weapon states being in a position to frustrate it, on the model of the chemical and biological weapons conventions where a legal norm was first adopted and practical abolition followed. This event culminated in October 2016 in a successful vote in the First Committee of the General Assembly to convene in 2017 a United Nations conference to negotiate a legally binding instrument to prohibit nuclear weapons.[18] Secondly, the OEWG will 'make recommendations on *other measures*' to increase transparency about nuclear risks and especially, to reduce and eliminate the risk of accidental, mistaken, unauthorized or intentional nuclear weapons detonations'. This refers to long-standing calls from the NPT membership for nuclear weapon states to reduce the salience of nuclear weapons in their national security doctrines and strategies and to reduce the risks of nuclear use by measures such as de-alerting weapons, eliminating MIRVs and adopting 'no first use' and 'sole use' postures. It is a clear statement that the international community has an interest in the way that states posture their nuclear forces and incorporate them into national security and military doctrine. This agenda raises the question of how nuclear weapon states can practically move to reduce and then eliminate their nuclear arsenals without prejudicing their own security while doing so. Creative thinking about how this can occur is discussed below.

On non-proliferation, a different divide emerges. This has arisen because of the experience of a number of states abusing the rights embodied in Articles X and IV of the NPT (to exit and peaceful uses) to flout the non-proliferation objectives of the treaty and begin developing nuclear weapons. This

can also be said of those countries who did not join the NPT –
Israel, India, Pakistan, South Africa (who joined in 1991),
France and China (who joined in 1992) – but did exploit the
civilian trade in nuclear technology established following the
atoms for peace programme. Some Western states are keen
to limit the interpretation of peaceful uses of nuclear energy,
by limiting the abilities of states to enrich uranium through
what is termed the 'multi-lateralization of the nuclear fuel
cycle' (colloquially known as the nuclear 'fuel bank'). While
there are many different proposals under discussion, it would
guarantee states access to low-enriched nuclear fuel for power
and medical reactors while limiting or denying their capacity
to enrich uranium and produce nuclear fuel domestically.[19]

The 120 state members of the Non-Aligned Movement, in
contrast, stated in a working paper to the 2015 Revcon that
they reject 'any attempt aimed at discouraging certain peaceful
nuclear activities on the grounds of their alleged "sensitivity"'
and assert that every member of the NPT 'has a sovereign
right to define its national energy and fuel-cycle policies,
which, inter alia, includes an inalienable right to develop, for
peaceful purposes, a full national nuclear fuel cycle'. This is,
arguably, a tendentious interpretation of Article IV which
states: 'nothing in this Treaty shall be interpreted as affecting
the inalienable right of all the Parties to the Treaty to develop
research, production and use of nuclear energy for peaceful
purposes without discrimination'. The NAM view is somewhat shortsighted, given that strong international control
of the nuclear fuel cycle will be an essential condition of the
elimination of nuclear weapons; that, as we transition to a
'zero' world governed by a Nuclear Weapons Convention, this
assumption about the NPT bargain will have to be modified.[20]
The NAM indicate that they will continue to engage in discussions about fuel-cycle multi-lateralization but there is obvious
suspicion and a strong refusal to revisit that ambiguous and

problematic element of the NPT bargain. Divisions also are visible around long-standing proposals for a Fissile Material Cutoff Treaty (FMCT), with the Non-aligned Movement promoting it strongly, newer nuclear states outside the NPT being opposed, and the nuclear weapon states supporting a ban on future production but being ambivalent about giving up their existing stocks.[21]

In sum, the fractures appearing on both sides of the NPT bargain threaten to weaken dramatically the thick connective tissue between them. If proliferation, whether upwards in numbers or outwards to more states, is to be held back, efforts at disarmament must pick up momentum. This is a message that is repeated often by NPT member states and was set out in the 2010 NPT Revcon outcome, which emphasized the Treaty's 'shared objectives of the total elimination of nuclear weapons, [and] preventing, under any circumstances, the further proliferation of nuclear weapons'.[22] The 2009 International Commission on Nuclear Non-Proliferation and Disarmament (ICNND) put the case eloquently: 'So long as any state has nuclear weapons, others will want them. So long as any such weapons remain, it defies credibility that they will not one day be used, by accident, miscalculation or design . . . maintaining the status quo is not an option.'[23]

Moving towards zero

In 1995, 2000 and 2010, the member states of the NPT unequivocally asserted the Treaty's requirement for complete nuclear abolition. This was stated starkly in the 2010 Review Conference outcome:

> The Conference notes the reaffirmation by the nuclear-weapon States of their unequivocal undertaking to accomplish, in accordance with the principle of irreversibility, the total elimination of their nuclear arsenals leading to nuclear

disarmament, to which all States parties are committed under article VI of the Treaty.[24]

The question then is how this can and should be done. Moving towards and then completing the elimination of nuclear weapons is technically, strategically and politically complex. However, it is achievable. Opponents raise a range of objections: nuclear weapons cannot be uninvented; the international security context is not (or will never be) conducive; unilateral disarmament is unwise; nuclear disarmament will lead to more conventional wars; total elimination cannot be effectively verified, policed or enforced, and the risk of cheating is too great; or the anarchic and conflictual nature of international relations will have to radically change. Some of these arguments raise serious problems that many analysts have sought to address thoughtfully. Others are self-serving rhetoric from supporters of the nuclear weapon states, behind which lies the less honourable and unstated belief that nuclear weapons remain useful for national defence, prestige and power, and the global security interest be damned. It is sadder when organizations established to promote serious thinking about a path to zero, such as the ICNND, repeat some of this thinking, which is touched on below.[25]

Even if NPT member states have not dedicated significant resources to the problem of getting to zero, there is rich and advanced thinking available. Following on from some creative long-range thinking by Jonathan Schell in the 1980s, a series of studies and reports have set out a viable and realistic path towards nuclear abolition and shown that the outstanding dilemmas can be resolved. The International Institute for Strategic Studies (IISS) has published three major studies on the strategic and governance complexities of deep nuclear reductions and abolition, by George Perkovitch and James Acton, David Cortwright and Raimo Väyrynen, and James

Acton.[26] The Carnegie Endowment for International Peace has also built on these studies and promoted further debate.[27] Most significantly, an international commission of eminent persons and former policy-makers – the ICNND – drew on many of these studies to set out a staged path for deep nuclear disarmament and eventual abolition, in a major report that was widely circulated at the 2010 NPT Review Conference.[28] These papers and the ICNND report discuss how strategic stability and deterrence can be maintained during the disarmament process, how concerns about verification and cheating can be addressed and disarmament enforced and how concerns about conventional warfare and insecurity can also be addressed without letting them be a barrier to nuclear disarmament.

Without prejudicing the debate within and between these publications, it is possible to identify an emerging consensus. Firstly, nuclear disarmament would not be unilateral or conducted in a way that neglects the legitimate (as opposed to the more spurious) national security concerns of existing nuclear states. Rather it would be cooperative, negotiated, and staged with the ideal of preserving strategic stability and building confidence at all stages. It would begin with the USA and Russia negotiating bilateral arms control beyond New START to achieve a 'minimization point' of around five hundred warheads each, with other nuclear states possessing about half that number or less. This would be accompanied by interim supporting measures such as strengthening controls on nuclear testing and fissile materials (with the CTBT and FMCT coming into force and progress on multi-lateralization of the nuclear fuel cycle), measures to reduce the salience of nuclear weapons in national security policy and reduce the risks of intended or accidental use, and to strengthen IAEA safeguards and other non-proliferation institutions. These interim measures are now a commonplace demand of NPT

Review Conferences and other meetings. Once the minimization point is reached, the other nuclear states can be engaged so that mutual reductions toward zero can be progressed.

To support and maintain the transition to zero, enhanced and strengthened forms of verification, surveillance, intelligence and enforcement will need to be developed and operated cooperatively. These will be important as states move to low numbers and thence to abolition. A range of ideas are under discussion – from enhanced powers for the IAEA to conduct 'anywhere, anytime' inspections, and stronger cooperation between it and national intelligence agencies (what is known as 'end-to-end verification'), to a return to the immediate post-war notion of a single world nuclear agency that also has control of weapons and production facilities, as was envisaged in the Acheson–Lilienthal report.[29] My view is that enhanced and effective powers for the IAEA will be the bare minimum to cope with a substantially disarmed or nuclear weapons free world and that policy-makers should be open to more ambitious concepts ('world nuclear government') that would secure the common peace. Such strengthened verification, supported by effective enforcement, will assuage the concerns that a state may seek to cheat, or 'break out', by stealthily reconstituting hidden or dismantled weapons and then trying to blackmail other states with them. Whether such blackmail would actually work is a strategically salient question and should not be assumed; however the key objective must be to prevent such a situation arising at all.

There is also now some creative strategic thinking about how to secure a world with very few or no nuclear weapons. Some analysts speak of a 'vantage point' of very low numbers (50–100 each) in which one can imagine there are minimal defensive deployments, as is the case in the United Kingdom now. From there, zero can be seen and aimed for. However what 'zero' would mean in reality is still under discussion. One concept is the 'virtual arsenal', in which warheads and delivery systems are kept intact and functional but are de-mated – separated, for example, by hundreds of kilometres and placed under international supervision. Another is 'weaponless deterrence' in which nuclear weapons are dismantled entirely and production facilities rendered weapons-incapable and placed under strict safeguards, but the knowledge of how to build and deploy nuclear weapons remains as a final level of deterrence to cheating or large-scale conventional aggression. Interestingly, it is also suggested that ballistic missile defences may be established after abolition – but not a moment before – as another layer of reassurance in the face of mutual vulnerability.[30] One can imagine how desirable it would be to abolish nuclear weapons absolutely – materials, weapons, knowledge – but this would be the point at which we must acknowledge that nuclear weapons cannot be uninvented, if for the basic fact that the underlying physics that made them possible is by now widely known.

There are concerns that very low numbers would be a somewhat nerve-racking stage.[31] In my view, it should not be allowed to solidify into an ongoing situation, but should merely be a phase that is passed through (perhaps through staged multi-lateral assessments of rough parity) on the way to zero. The very strong verification and enforcement architecture that will be required at zero will also need to be in place *before* nuclear weapon states reach low numbers, as a system of assurance that will enable them to confidently pass through that phase to abolition. It is also a phase where there would need to be general commitment to the view that nuclear weapons are illegitimate and cannot be used and that the fundamental responsibility of states-persons and soldiers responsible for them is to manage the process of total abolition.

In 2016 it is obvious that such a future is hard to see, even if a range of compelling analyses have shown that it is possible and that all of the potential strategic and tactical problems that may arise can be surmounted. Here it is important to comment on one area of disagreement in this debate – the issue of conventional arms imbalances and national defence without nuclear weapons. We should question the opinion, which was expressed by the ICNND in its report, that moving beyond the minimization point to a nuclear weapons free world would 'require the transformation of the existing international relations system'. The Commission defined such a transformation as involving successful efforts to:

> create cooperative geopolitical conditions, regionally and globally, [that] mak[e] the prospect of major war or aggression so remote that nuclear weapons are seen as having no remaining deterrent utility . . . all outstanding territorial disputes and other potential sources of major conflict . . . are resolved, or at least that the status quo has become comfortable enough for all sides.[32]

Such an opinion confuses two things: the perceived utility of nuclear weapons against conventional threats, otherwise known as asymmetric deterrence; and the additional vulnerability some states may feel if they have to rely on conventional weapons alone for their national defence. These are certainly relevant considerations given that they represent widely held views that reach into current defence and national security doctrines. However they are based on mistaken and dangerous perspectives. The better news is that they can begin to be addressed immediately and efforts to do so are visible in international meetings. What is required is a creative combination of arms control measures and improved thinking that can quarantine nuclear weapons from conventional conflict and provide states with mutual reassurance.

Two issues must be unpacked here. Firstly, an argument that all major conflicts must first be resolved and the fundamental dynamics of international relations changed is tantamount to saying that nuclear weapons can never really be abolished. Against this, I would argue that global security will only be achieved by fundamentally disconnecting nuclear weapons and conventional conflict, rather than clinging to the Cold War canard that the presence of nuclear threats somehow prevented major interstate war. The historical record does not support this view and it burdens humanity with an appalling level of risk for a debatable outcome. Deploying nuclear weapons as a conventional deterrent creates extraordinarily dangerous risks of escalation to nuclear war in a crisis or during a conventional war. Strategists often refuse to admit the fact that nuclear weapons – because of their fundamental immorality and indiscriminate effects – cannot be used in warfare and therefore their utility as a deterrent to conventional conflict (or a decisive weapon within it) has to come into serious question. As was discussed in Chapter 3, this was exactly the anxiety that prevented American commanders from agreeing to the use of nuclear weapons during the Korean War and which prevented the Kennedy administration from invading Cuba during the missile crisis, given its frightening escalatory potential. It is however possible to promote foreign policies and forms of global security governance – such as the UN Security Council becoming more constructively engaged in efforts to reduce interstate strategic tensions and arms racing – that will control conventional interstate security dilemmas and reduce the amount that states need to spend on defence.

Secondly, if aggressively realist policies can become a 'self-fulfilling prophecy' by creating the very hostilities they assume, the reverse can be true. Reassuring, prudent and stabilizing policies can reduce insecurity and support the disarmament process. As Acton and Perkovich argue after William Walker, 'nuclear abolition [can] be approached as a "co-evolutionary" process of reciprocal step-by-step progress, in which non-proliferation and arms-reduction measures emerge from changed political and security environments and vice versa'.[33] In short, disarmament and national security can be reinforcing processes. Mutual disarmament will help reduce the sense of vulnerability and tension between nuclear adversaries and deepen a spirit of cooperation and mutual interest that will help resolve other issues and improve understanding. And even where significant conflict or tensions may continue, mature moral and strategic leadership will keep the collective benefits of nuclear abolition at the forefront of foreign policy and nuclear matters will be kept separate from other areas of international relations. In a world where interstate military aggression is prohibited by the UN Charter and will soon be an international crime, we should have more confidence that there is more keeping the peace than conventional arms balances and deterrence.

A change in thinking and doctrine is required. Too many states – among them Russia, France and Pakistan – have expansive and ambiguous nuclear doctrines that take in a range of contingencies including conventional warfare or the threat of biological weapons use. These are both profoundly destabilizing now and act as a significant barrier to deep nuclear reductions and disarmament in future. There are strong arguments for all the nuclear weapon states to be pressured to adopt three crucial measures: that they will not be the first to use nuclear weapons ('no first use'); that the sole purpose of nuclear weapons is to deter nuclear attack ('sole use'); and that non-nuclear weapon states will never be targeted with nuclear weapons ('negative security assurances'). Only China and India have declared no first use policies, while the USA and the UK have published formulations which come close. However the stabilizing and reassuring effect that such declarations would have cannot be underestimated. These should be paired with efforts to deal with those conventional capabilities under development which may be genuinely strategically destabilizing: here the most salient concerns are ballistic missile defence (BMD), which both Russia and China fear could eventually negate their deterrent; and US development of 'prompt global strike' long-range conventionally armed ballistic missile technology. It has been suggested that conventional ballistic missiles should be counted in nuclear arms control and disarmament and then banned as a part of nuclear abolition.[34] Similarly, the major powers could agree a new ABM treaty which permits research on BMD but forbids its deployment until nuclear abolition has been achieved.

This book has traced the very complex and dangerous world that the discovery and exploitation of the uranium atom has brought us. The current stalemate around nuclear weapons and disarmament is probably the most portentous and difficult result of that discovery. A large industry of policy-making, diplomacy, defence contracting and policy analysis has been built around either perpetuating or trying to resolve this stalemate. We are presented now with a somewhat bitter paradox: even as humanity and planet Earth itself remain threatened by the nuclear weaponry and thinking that still exists, there are promising signs of the diplomatic momentum and creative thinking that can lead us into a more hopeful future.

Notes

1 The Politics of Uranium

1 William Hague, 'Preventing a New Age of Nuclear Insecurity', speech to the International Institute of Strategic Studies, 23 July 2008, available at: http://www.iiss.org/recent-key-addresses/william-hague-address-jul-o8/; Joint statement by President Medvedev and President Obama, 1 April 2009, available at: http://www.armscontrol.org/node/3611.

2 Gar Alperovitz, *The Decision to Use the Atomic Bomb and the Architecture of an American Myth* (Knopf, 1995); 'Correspondence: Marshall, Truman and the decision to drop the bomb', Gar Alperovitz and Robert L. Messer, Barton J. Bernstein, *International Security*, 16(3), Winter 1990/91, 204–21.

3 Jeremy Bernstein, *Plutonium: A History of the World's Most Dangerous Element* (Sydney: NewSouth and Cornell University Press, 2009), 34.

4 World Nuclear Association, 'Supply of uranium', August 2012. http://www.world-nuclear.org/info/Nuclear-Fuel-Cycle/Uranium-Resources/Supply-of-Uranium/.

5 Richard L. Garwin and Georges Charpak, *Megawatts and Megatons: The Future of Nuclear Power and Nuclear Weapons* (Chicago: University of Chicago Press, 2002), 210–11.

6 Independent Investigation Commission on the Fukushima Nuclear Accident, *The Fukushima Daiichi Nuclear Power Station Disaster* (London and New York: Routledge, 2014).

7 David S. McDonough, 'Nuclear Superiority: The "New Triad" and the Evolution of Nuclear Strategy', *Adelphi Paper*, 383, 2006.

8 Bruno Latour, *Reassembling the Social: An Introduction to*

Actor-Network-Theory (Oxford and New York: Oxford University Press, 2007), pp. 54, 74; Mike Bourne, 'Guns don't kill people, cyborgs do: A Latourian Provocation for transformatory arms control and disarmament', *Global Change, Peace and Security*, 24(1), 2012, 141–63.

9   Anthony Burke, 'Nuclear time: temporal metaphors of the nuclear present', *Critical Studies on Security*, 4(1), 2016, 73–90; Tom Lundborg and Nick Vaughan-Williams, 'New Materialisms, Discourse Analysis, and International Relations: A Radical Intertextual Approach', *Review of International Studies*, 41(1), 2015, 3–25.

10 Lawrence Freedman, *The Evolution of Nuclear Strategy*, 3rd edn (Basingstoke: Palgrave Macmillan, 2003).

11 Anthony Burke, 'Nuclear reason: At the limits of strategy', *International Relations*, 23(4), 2009, 506–29.

12 *Treaty on the Non-Proliferation of Nuclear Weapons*, 1968. United Nations Office for Disarmament Affairs, Treaty Database. http://disarmament.un.org/treaties/t/npt/text

13 Mlada Bukovansky, Ian Clark, Robyn Eckersley, Richard Price, Christian Reus-Smit and Nicholas J. Wheeler, *Special Responsibilities: Global Problems and American Power* (Cambridge and New York: Cambridge University Press, 2012), 83, 87. See also, Reaching Critical Will, *Negative Security Assurances*. http://www.reachingcriticalwill.org/resources/fact-sheets/critical-issues/5442-negative-security-assurances

14 Kingston Reif, 'States clash on disarmament at UN', *Arms Control Today*. December 2014. http://www.armscontrol.org/ACT/2014_12/News/States-Clash-on-Disarmament-at-UN

15 *NPT*, Article III; IAEA, 'Additional Protocol'. https://www.iaea.org/safeguards/safeguards-legal-framework/additional-protocol

16 Mark Fitzpatrick, *Overcoming Pakistan's Nuclear Dangers*. Adelphi Paper 443 (London and New York: IISS and Routledge, 2014), 142–3.

17 Gareth Evans and Yoriko Kawaguchi, co-chairs, *Eliminating Nuclear Threats: A Practical Agenda for Global Policymakers* (Canberra and Tokyo: International Commission on Nuclear Non-Proliferation and Disarmament, 2009), 94.

18 Fitzpatrick, *Overcoming Pakistan's Nuclear Dangers*, 82–3; see also Gerald Warburg, 'Nonproliferation policy crossroads:

lessons learned from the US–India Cooperation Agreement', *The Nonproliferation Review*, 19(3), 2012, 451–71.

19 Damian Carrington, 'The Anthropocene epoch: scientists declare dawn of human-influenced age', *Guardian*, 29 August 2016. https://www.theguardian.com/environment/2016/ aug/29/declare-anthropocene-epoch-experts-urge-geological-congress-human-impact-earth.

2 THE BRIEF HISTORY OF A RESOURCE

1 Bernstein, *Plutonium*, 32; Garwin and Charpak, *Megawatts and Megatons*, 20–21.
2 David Holloway, *Stalin and the Bomb* (New Haven and London: Yale University Press, 1994), 50.
3 Holloway, *Stalin and the Bomb*, 57.
4 Gerard J. DeGroot, *The Bomb: A Life* (Cambridge, MA: Harvard University Press, 2004), 26.
5 Walter Isaacson, *Einstein: His Life and Universe* (New York: Simon and Schuster, 2007), 472.
6 DeGroot, *The Bomb*, 69; Anthony Burke, 'Nuclear reason: at the limits of strategy', *International Relations*, 23(9), 2009, 506–29.
7 DeGroot, *The Bomb*, 24.
8 Garwin and Charpak, *Megawatts and Megatons*, 26–7.
9 DeGroot, *The Bomb*, 53.
10 Tom Zoellner, *Uranium: War, Energy and the Rock that Shaped the World* (London: Viking, 2009), 18.
11 *The Delphi Complete Works of Hesiod*, Kindle edition. Loc 122.
12 Zoellner, *Uranium*, 17; Bertrand Goldschmidt, 'Uranium's scientific history 1789–1939', Paper presented to the Fourteenth International Symposium held by the Uranium Institute in London, September 1989. http://ist-socrates.berkeley. edu/~rochlin/ushist.html
13 Goldschmidt, 'Uranium's scientific history'.
14 Zoellner, *Uranium*, 5, 48–9; De Groot, *The Bomb*, 54; Holloway, *Stalin and the Bomb*, 111.
15 Zoellner, *Uranium*, 55; Holloway, *Stalin and the Bomb*, 174.
16 Mark Fitzpatrick, *Overcoming Pakistan's Nuclear Dangers*, Adelphi Paper 443 (London and New York: IISS and Routledge, 2014), 15.

17 Holloway, *Stalin and the Bomb*, 96, 63.
18 Ibid., 175–6, 193–4; Joseph Cirincione, *Bomb Scare: The History and Future of Nuclear Weapons* (New York: Columbia University Press, 2007), 36.
19 Richard Rhodes, *The Making of the Atomic Bomb* (New York and London: Simon and Schuster, 2012). Kindle edition. Loc 6292.
20 Alex Wellerstein, 'The price of the Manhattan project', *Restricted Data: The Nuclear Secrecy Blog*, 17 May 2013. http://blog.nuclear secrecy.com/2013/05/17/the-price-of-the-manhattan-project/
21 Wellerstein, 'The price of the Manhattan project'.
22 Kai Bird and Martin J. Sherwin, *American Prometheus. The Triumph and Tragedy of J. Robert Oppenheimer* (London and New York: Vintage, 2006), 284; Joseph Rotblat, 'Leaving the bomb project', *The Bulletin of the Atomic Scientists*, August 1985, 17.
23 Bird and Sherwin, *American Prometheus*, 287.
24 Ibid., 289.
25 J. Robert Oppenheimer, *Uncommon Sense* (Boston: Birkhauser, 1984).
26 DeGroot, *The Bomb: A Life*, 68.
27 Bird and Sherwin, *American Prometheus*, 298.
28 McGeorge Bundy, *Danger And Survival: Choices About The Bomb In The First Fifty Years* (New York: Vintage, 1988), 70.
29 Ibid., 67.
30 Bird and Sherwin, *American Prometheus*, 291–3, 297. A copy of the Franck report is available at the Federation of American Scientists: http://www.fas.org/sgp/eprint/franck.html
31 DeGroot, *The Bomb: A Life*, 77. For more on the targeting committee and especially the debate over Kyoto, see: http://blog.nuclearsecrecy.com/2014/08/08/kyoto-misconception/
32 John H. Else, Dir. 'The Day After Trinity'. KTEH Television. 1980. Timecode: 57:26.
33 Bundy, *Danger And Survival*, 60.
34 Ibid., 64–6.
35 Protocol Additional to the Geneva Conventions of 12 August 1949 and relating to the Protection of Victims of International Armed Conflicts (Protocol I), 8 June 1977. Article 51(5)(a).
36 Heinz Marcus Hanke, 'The 1923 Hague Rules of Air Warfare: A contribution to the development of international law protecting civilians from air attack', *International Review of the Red Cross*, 33, 1993, 12–44.

37 Errol Morris Dir. *The Fog of War*, Sony Pictures Classics. 2003.

38 Paul Ham, *Hiroshima and Nagasaki: The Real Story of the Atomic Bombings and their Aftermath* (London: Doubleday, 2012), Loc. 5514.

39 Ibid., loc. 5500, 5678.

40 Ibid., loc 6263.

41 Ibid., loc 7079.

42 Ibid., loc 6165, 6220, 6958, 7173–79.

43 Ibid., loc. 5902, 5994.

44 Ibid., loc. 6050, 6063, 6573.

45 Gar Alperovitz, 'Did we have to drop the bomb?', *The New York Times*, 3 August 1989, A23; see also Gar Alperovitz, *The Decision to Use the Atomic Bomb and the Architecture of an American Myth* (Knopf, 1995).

46 Ham, *Hiroshima and Nagasaki*, loc. 6066.

47 Bundy, *Danger and Survival*, 82–97 and 'Correspondence: Marshall, Truman and the decision to drop the bomb', Gar Alperovitz and Robert L. Messer, Barton J. Bernstein, *International Security*, 16(3), Winter 1990/91, 204–21.

48 Bird and Sherwin, *American Prometheus*, 273.

49 The '*Franck' Report: A Report to the Secretary of War*, June 1945. Available at The Federation of American Scientists, http://fas. org/sgp/eprint/franck.html. Viewed 12 March 2015.

50 The Acheson–Lilienthal Report – Report on the International Control of Atomic Energy, March 16, 1946. http://www. learnworld.com/ZNW/LWText.Acheson-Lilienthal. html#page25; A photocopy of the report can be found at: http:// www.foia.cia.gov/sites/default/files/document_conversions/50/ Report_on_the_International_Control_of_Atomic_Energy_16_ Mar_1946.PDF

51 Randy Rydell, 'Going for Baruch: The Nuclear Plan That Refused to Go Away', *Arms Control Today*, 1 June 2006. http:// www.armscontrol.org/print/2064 Viewed 12 March 2015.

52 Ibid..

53 Bernard Brodie, 'Implications for Military Policy', in Bernard Brodie ed., *The Absolute Weapon: Atomic Power and World Order* (New York: Harcourt and Brace, 1946), 76.

3 WEAPONS AND SECURITY

1 Lawrence Freedman, *The Evolution of Nuclear Strategy* (London: Palgrave Macmillan, 2003), ch. 25.
2 Colin S. Gray and Keith Payne, 'Victory Is Possible', *Foreign Policy*, 39, 1980, 21.
3 Schlosser, *Command and Control*, 448–9; Patricia Lewis, Heather Williams, Benoît Pelopidas and Sasan Aghlani, *Too Close for Comfort: Cases of Near Nuclear Use and Options for Policy* (London: Chatham House, April 2014), 13–16.
4 William Walker, *A Perpetual Menace: Nuclear Weapons and International Order* (London and New York: Routledge, 2010).
5 Hans J. Morgenthau, 'The Four Paradoxes of Nuclear Strategy'. *American Political Science Review*, 58(1), 1964, 23–35; Anthony Burke, 'Nuclear Reason: At the Limits of Strategy'. *International Relations* 23(4), 2009, 506–29.
6 For a list of such figures see McNamara and Blight, *Wilson's Ghost*, 203–7. See also George P. Shultz, William J. Perry, Henry A. Kissinger and Sam Nunn, 'Deterrence in the Age of Nuclear Proliferation', *The Wall Street Journal*, 7 March 2011 and the report of the *Global Zero Commission on Nuclear Risk Reduction*. http://www.globalzero.org/get-the-facts/nuclear-risk-reduction
7 ILPI, 'Evidence of Catastrophe: A summary of the facts presented at the three conferences on the humanitarian impact of nuclear weapons', International Law And Policy Institute, Background Paper, 15, 2015. http://nwp.ilpi.org/?p=3388 *See also Conference Report*, Vienna Conference on the Humanitarian Impact of Nuclear Weapons 8–9 December 2014 (Vienna: Federal Ministry for Europe, Integration and Foreign Affairs, 2015).
8 A copy of the statement is available at: http://www.bmeia.gv.at/fileadmin/user_upload/Zentrale/Aussenpolitik/Abruestung/HINW14/HINW14_Message_from_His_Holiness_Pope_Francis.pdf
9 The UNGA statement presented by New Zealand can be found at: http://www.un.org/disarmament/special/meetings/firstcommittee/68/pdfs/TD_21-Oct_CL-1_New_Zealand-Joint_St The 'Humanitarian Pledge' can be found at: http://www.bmeia.gv.at/fileadmin/user_upload/Zentrale/

Aussenpolitik/Abruestung/HINW14/HINW14vienna_Pledge_
Document.pdf

10 Scott D. Sagan and Kenneth N. Waltz, *The Spread Of Nuclear
Weapons: An Enduring Debate*, 3rd edition (New York and
London: W. W. Norton, 2013), 4; Kenneth Waltz, 'The Virtue of
Adversity', *International Relations*, 23(3), 2009, 501.

11 Bernard Brodie, 'War in the Atomic Age', in Bernard Brodie
(ed.), *The Absolute Weapon: Atomic Power and World Order*
(New York: Harcourt and Brace, 1946), p. 23.

12 Sergey Radchenko, 'Did Hiroshima save Japan from
Soviet occupation?', *Foreign Policy*, 5 August 2015. https://
foreignpolicy.com/2015/08/05/stalin_japan_hiroshima_
occupation_hokkaido/?curator=MediaREDEF

13 Freedman, *The Evolution of Nuclear Strategy*, 58; Holloway,
Stalin and the Bomb, 305–6.

14 Rhodes, *Dark Sun*, loc. 4825–42, 7682.

15 Ibid., loc. 7082.

16 Freedman, *The Evolution of Nuclear Strategy*, 72; Rhodes, *Dark
Sun*, loc 7107.

17 DeGroot, *The Bomb*, 185–188; Rhodes, *Dark Sun*, loc. 9998,
10130; Conrad Crane, 'Searching for Lucrative Targets in North
Korea: The Shift from Interdiction to Air Pressure', in Jacob
Neufeld and George M. Watson Jr eds. Coalition Air Warfare
in the Korean War, 1950–1953, *Proceedings of the Air Force
Historical Foundation Symposium*, Andrews AFB, Maryland, 7–8
May 2002, 158–77.

18 Holloway, *Stalin and the Bomb*, 299.

19 Garwin and Charpak, *Megawatts and Megatons*, 61–2; Holloway,
Stalin and the Bomb, 307.

20 Garwin and Charpak, *Megawatts and Megatons*, 62–3.

21 Nuclear Weapon Archive. http://nuclearweaponarchive.org/
Usa/Weapons/Allbombs.html Accessed 11/9/15.

22 Nuclear Weapon Archive; Effects and casualty estimates taken
from the Nuclear Secrecy 'NukeMap3D' simulation, http://
nuclearsecrecy.com/nukemap3d/# Accessed 13/9/15.

23 Holloway, *Stalin and the Bomb*, 322, 308; Hans M. Kristensen
and Robert S. Norris, 'Nuclear notebook: Global nuclear
weapons inventories, 1945–2013', *Bulletin of the Atomic
Scientists*, 69(5), 75–81.

24 Rhodes, *Dark Sun*, loc. 10535, 12197.

25 Ibid., loc. 9030.
26 Ibid., loc. 9162.
27 Bundy, *Danger and Survival*, 213.
28 Ibid., 214, 220.
29 William Bundy, *A Tangled Web: The Making of Foreign Policy in the Nixon Presidency* (New York: Hill and Wang, 1998), pp. 88–100.
30 Holloway, *Stalin and the Bomb*, 336–9.
31 Harry S. Truman, 'State of the Union 1953 - 7 January 1953'. http://www.let.rug.nl/usa/presidents/harry-s-truman/state-of-the-union-1953.php
32 950 B36 bombs, each with a yield of 10 Mt, were retired from service in 1961. Rhodes, *Dark Sun*, loc. 9030; Nuclear Notebook, 'Estimated U.S. And Soviet/Russian Nuclear Stockpiles 1945–94', *The Bulletin of the Atomic Scientists*, November–December 1994, 59.
33 Freedman, *The Evolution of Nuclear Strategy*, 71–84.
34 Holloway, *Stalin and the Bomb*, 328.
35 Kristensen and Norris, 'Nuclear notebook: Global nuclear weapons inventories', 78.
36 Rhodes, *Dark Sun*, loc. 12608, 12674; Holloway, *Stalin and the Bomb*, 332, 342.
37 J. Robert Oppenheimer, 'Atomic Weapons And American Policy', *Foreign Affairs*, 31(4), July 1953, 529.
38 Bundy, *Danger and Survival*, 381.
39 Sheldon M. Stern, *The Week the World Stood Still: Inside the Secret Cuban Missile Crisis* (Stanford University Press, 2005), 21; Bundy, *Danger and Survival*, 415–16.
40 Robert S. McNamara and James G. Blight, *Wilson's Ghost* (New York: Public Affairs, 2003), 189.
41 Scott D. Sagan, *The Limits of Safety: Organizations, Accidents, and Nuclear Weapons* (Princeton University Press, 1993), 117–20; Schlosser, *Command and Control*, 292.
42 John F. Kennedy, Address on the Cuban Crisis, 22 October 1962. https://legacy.fordham.edu/halsall/mod/1962kennedy-cuba.html.
43 McNamara and Blight, *Wilson's Ghost*, 189; Errol Morris Dir. *The Fog of War*, Sony Pictures Classics. 2003. Timestamp 17.08.
44 Sagan, *Limits of Safety*, 71–117.
45 Treaty Banning Nuclear Weapon Tests in the Atmosphere, in Outer Space and Under Water. Bureau of Arms Control,

Verification, and Compliance. US Department of State. http://www.state.gov/t/isn/4797.htm.

46 'The Status of the Comprehensive Test Ban Treaty: Signatories and Ratifiers', Arms Control Association. https://www.armscontrol.org/factsheets/ctbtsig.

47 Freedman, *The Evolution of Nuclear Strategy*, 222–230; Peter Pringle and William Arkin, *SIOP: Nuclear War From the Inside* (London: Sphere Books, 1983), 87–92.

48 A copy of the agreement is held at: http://www.state.gov/www/global/arms/treaties/abm/abm2.html.

49 A copy of the treaty is archived at: http://www.un.org/disarmament/WMD/Nuclear/NPTtext.shtml.

50 Nuclear Notebook, 'Estimated U.S. And Soviet/Russian Nuclear Stockpiles'; Hans M. Kristensen and Robert S. Norris, 'Nuclear notebook: Global nuclear weapons inventories, 1945–2013', 78; Desmond Ball, 'The Development of the SIOP, 1960–1983', in Desmond Ball and Jeffrey Richelson (eds), *Strategic Nuclear Targeting* (Ithaca, NY: Cornell University Press, 1987), 75.

51 R. P. Turco, O. B. Toon, T. P. Ackerman, J. B. Pollack, C. Sagan, 'Climate and Smoke: An Appraisal of Nuclear Winter', *Science*, 247, 12 January 1990.

52 Alan Robock, Luke Oman, Georgiy L. Stenchikov, Owen B. Toon, Charles Bardeen and Richard P. Turco, 'Climatic consequences of regional nuclear conflicts', *Atmospheric Chemistry and Physics*, Vol. 7, 2007, 2003–2012; Alan Robock, Luke Oman and Georgiy L. Stenchikov, 'Nuclear winter revisited with a modern climate model and current nuclear arsenals: Still catastrophic consequences', *Journal of Geophysical Research – Atmospheres*, 112 (D13), 2007.

53 Carl Sagan, 'Nuclear Winter: Nuclear War would be an Unprecedented Human Catastrophe', *Global Research*, 9 November 2010. http://www.globalresearch.ca/nuclear-winter-nuclear-war-would-be-an-unprecedented-human-catastrophe/21840

54 Freedman, *The Evolution of Nuclear Strategy*, 388.

55 Desmond Ball and Robert C. Toth, 'Revising the SIOP: Taking War-Fighting to Dangerous Extremes', *International Security*, 14(4), 1990, 86; Michael Howard, 'On Fighting Nuclear War', *International Security*, 5(4), 1981, 17.

56 Lewis, et. al., *Too Close for Comfort*, 12,15; *Global Zero Commission On Nuclear Risk Reduction: De-Alerting and*

Stabilizing the World's Nuclear Force Postures, April 2015, 20.
http://www.globalzero.org/get-the-facts/nuclear-risk-reduction

57 See Dennis M. Gormley, Patricia M. Lewis, Miles A.
Pomper, Lawrence Scheinman, Stephen Schwartz, Nikolai
Sokov, Leonard S. Spector, *Four Emerging Issues in Arms
Control, Disarmament, and Nonproliferation: Opportunities for
German Leadership*, Prepared for the Policy Planning Staff,
Foreign Office, Federal Republic of Germany (Monterey:
James Martin Center for Nonproliferation Studies, 2009).
Available at: http://www.isn.ethz.ch/Digital-Library/
Publications/Detail/?ots591=0c54e3b3-1e9c-be1e-2c24-
a6a8c7060233&lng=en&id=116403

58 'Vladimir Putin issues new "large nuclear power" warning to
West', *The Telegraph*, 29 September 2015. http://www.telegraph.
co.uk/news/worldnews/vladimir-the putin/11167192/Vladimir-
Putin-issues-new-large-nuclear-power-warning-to-West.html
Secretary-General's message to the Opening Plenary of the
Treaty on the Non-Proliferation of Nuclear Weapons [delivered
by the Deputy Secretary-General Jan Eliasson], New York,
27 April 2015. http://www.un.org/sg/statements/index.
asp?nid=8581 Accessed 15 May 2015.

59 Bilyana Lilly, *Russian Foreign Policy toward Missile Defense:
Actors, Motivations, and Influence* (Lexington, 2014).

60 'General Overview of the Effects of Nuclear Testing', CTBTO
Preparatory Commission. https://www.ctbto.org/nuclear-
testing/the-effects-of-nuclear-testing/general-overview-of-
theeffects-of-nuclear-testing/

61 Frank Walker, *Maralinga* (Sydney: Hachette, 2014), 151–5.

62 Karl Matheison, 'Losing paradise: the people displaced by
atomic bombs, and now climate change',*Guardian*, 10 March
2015. http://www.theguardian.com/environment/2015/
mar/09/losing-paradise-the-people-displaced-by-atomic-bombs-
and-now-climate-change

63 DeGroot, *The Bomb*, 197; Coleen Jose, Kim Wall and Jan
Hendrik Hinzel, 'This dome in the Pacific houses tons of
radioactive waste – and it's leaking', *Guardian*, 3 July 2015.
http://www.theguardian.com/world/2015/jul/03/runit-dome-
pacific-radioactive-waste

64 Annie Jacobsen, *Area 51: An Uncensored History of America's Top
Secret Military Base* (London: Orion, 2011), 119.

65 'United States Nuclear Testing', CTBTO Preparatory
    Commission. https://www.ctbto.org/nuclear-testing/the-
    effects-of-nuclear-testing/the-united-states-nuclear-testing-
    programme/

66 Angelique Chrisafis, 'French nuclear tests "showered vast area
    of Polynesia with radioactivity"', *Guardian*, 4 July 2013. http://
    www.theguardian.com/world/2013/jul/03/french-nuclear-tests-
    polynesia-declassified

67 Steven L. Simon, Andre Bouville and Charles E. Land, 'Fallout
    from Nuclear Weapons Tests and Cancer Risks', *American
    Scientist*, 94, January–February 2006; Charles E. Land, André
    Bouville, Iulian Apostoaei and Steven L. Simon, 'Projected
    Lifetime Cancer Risks From Exposure To Regional Radioactive
    Fallout In The Marshall Islands', *Health Physics*, 99(2), August
    2010, 105–23.

68 Lucy Westcott, 'Marshall Islands Nuclear Lawsuit Reopens
    Old Wounds', *Newsweek*, 8 January 2014. http://www.
    newsweek.com/marshall-islands-nuclear-lawsuit-reopens-old-
    wounds-262491 See also Lawyers Committee on Nuclear Policy
    Inc. http://www.lcnp.org/RMI/

69 Isobelle Gidley and Richard Shears, *The Rainbow Warrior Affair*
    (London: Unwin, 1986).

70 DeGroot, *The Bomb*, 199; 'Soviet Union Nuclear Testing',
    CTBTO Preparatory Commission. https://www.ctbto.org/
    nuclear-testing/the-effects-of-nuclear-testing/the-soviet-
    unionsnuclear-testing-programme/

71 Marianne Hanson, 'Nuclear Weapons as Obstacles to
    International Security', *International Relations*, 16(3), 2002,
    361; William Walker, 'Nuclear enlightenment and counter-
    enlightenment', *International Affairs*, 83(3), 2007, 431–53.

4 MINING, POLITICS AND PEOPLE

1   Barbara Rose Johnston, ed. *Half-lives and Half-truths:
    Confronting the Radioactive Legacies of the Cold War* (Santa Fe:
    School of Advanced Research Press, 2007), 1–24.

2   Geordan Graetz, 'Uranium Mining and First Peoples: The
    Nuclear Renaissance Confronts Historical Legacies', *Journal of
    Cleaner Production*, 84, 2014, 339–47.

3 Johnston, *Half-lives and Half-truths*, 2.

4 *Uranium 2014: Resources, Production and Demand*, OECD Nuclear Energy Agency and the International Atomic Energy Agency, 11–14.

5 'World Uranium Mining Production', World Nuclear Association. http://www.world-nuclear.org/information-library/nuclear-fuel-cycle/mining-of-uranium/world-uranium-mining-production.aspx Accessed 12 May 2016.

6 UxC Nuclear Fuel Price Indicators: https://www.uxc.com/p/prices/UxCPrices.aspx; UxC Historical Ux Price Charts: https://www.uxc.com/p/prices/UxCPriceChart.aspx?chart=spot-u3o8-full Accessed 19 June 2016.

7 James Conca, 'As the World Warms to Nuclear Power, the Outlook for Uranium is Up', *Forbes*, 4 January 2016. http://www.forbes.com/sites/jamesconca/2016/01/04/the-2016-uranium-market-reflecting-the-worldview-on-nuclear-power/#7faae7e43c6e Accessed 19 June 2016.

8 Vicky Validakis, 'Price collapse sees junior miner ditch uranium to focus on property development', *Australian Mining*, 6 June 2014. https://australianmining.com.au/news/price-collapse-sees-junior-miner-ditch-uranium-to-focus-on-property-development-2/ Accessed 19 June 2014.

9 'World Uranium Mining Production', World Nuclear Association. http://www.world-nuclear.org/information-library/nuclear-fuel-cycle/mining-of-uranium/world-uranium-mining-production.aspx.

10 Dr Gavin Mudd, 'In-Situ Leach (ISL) Uranium Mining Method Far From "Benign"', Friends of the Earth Australia, 2007. http://www.foe.org.au/anti-nuclear/issues/oz/u/isl/articles

11 Nuclear Suppliers Group, 'Guidelines for Nuclear Transfers', Part 1, June 2013.

12 'India-Australia agreement complete', *World Nuclear News*, 16 November 2015. http://www.world-nuclear-news.org/NP-India-Australia-agreement-complete-1611157.html.

13 Mark Fitzpatrick, *Overcoming Pakistan's Nuclear Dangers*. Adelphi Paper 443 (London and New York: IISS and Routledge, 2014), 57–8, 142–3.

14 Habil Frank Winde, 'Uranium pollution of water: a global perspective on the situation in South Africa', *Vaal Triangle*

Occasional Papers: Inaugural lecture 10/2013, Vanderbijlpark, 22 February 2013, 11.

15 Oliver Balch, 'Radioactive city: how Johannesburg's townships are paying for its mining past', *Guardian*, 6 July 2015. https://www.theguardian.com/cities/2015/jul/06/radioactive-city-how-johannesburgs-townships-are-paying-for-its-mining-past.

16 Nicholas R. Pederson, 'The French Desire for Uranium and its Effects on French Foreign Policy in Africa', *Arms Control, Disarmament, and International Security: Occasional Papers*. PED:1. University of Illinois at Urbana-Champaign, 2000.

17 Jacey Fortin, 'In Niger, New Disputes Over French Uranium Extraction', *International Business Times*, 6 February 2013.

18 Reuters, '3-Areva signs uranium deal with Niger, delays new mine', 26 May 2014. http://uk.reuters.com/article/areva-niger-idUKL6N0OC2TB20140526

19 WISE Uranium Project, 'New Uranium Mining Projects – Niger', http://www.wise-uranium.org/upne.html.

20 Environmental Justice Organizations, Liabilities and Trade (Ejolt), 'The radiological impact of uranium extraction in Northern Niger', 16 January 2015. http://www.ejolt.org/wordpress/wp-content/uploads/2015/02/FS_015_Niger-Uranium.pdf.

21 Shampa Biswas, *Nuclear Desire: Power and the Postcolonial Nuclear Order* (Minneapolis and London: University of Minnesota Press, 2014), loc. 3284.

22 Traci Brynne Voyles, *Wastelanding: Legacies of Uranium Mining in Navajo Country* (Minneapolis and London: University of Minnesota Press, 2015), loc. 405; see also Arn Keeling and John Sandlos, 'Environmental justice goes underground? Historical Notes from Canada's Northern Mining frontier', *Environmental Justice*, 2(3), 2009, 111–25.

23 Susan E. Dawson and Gary E. Madsen, 'Uranium mine workers, atomic downwinders, and the Radiation Exposure Compensation Act (RECA)' in Barbara Rose Johnston, ed. *Half-lives and Half-truths: Confronting the Radioactive Legacies of the Cold War* (Santa Fe: School of Advanced Research Press, 2007), 125–6.

24 Howard Ball, *Justice Downwind: America's Atomic Testing*

Program in the 1950s (Oxford and New York: Oxford University Press, 1986), 39.

25 Dawson and Madsen, 'Uranium mine workers', 125–33.

26 Stephanie A. Malin and Peggy Petrzelka, 'Left in the dust: Uranium's Legacy and victims of mill tailings exposure in Monticello Utah', *Society and Natural Resources*, 23, 2010, 1190–1193; Stephanie A. Malin and Peggy Petrzelka, 'Community development among toxic tailings: An interactional case study of extralocal institutions and environmental health', *Community Development*, 43(3), 2012, 385–6.

27 Stephanie A. Malin, *The Price of Nuclear Power: Uranium Communities and Environmental Justice* (New Brunswick: Rutgers University Press, 2015), 45–6, 68–71.

28 Malin, *The Price of Nuclear Power*, 75–7, 106–8; Arn Keeling, "Born in an atomic test tube': landscapes of cyclonic development at Uranium City, Saskatchewan', *The Canadian Geographer*, 54(2), 2010, 229–52.

29 Environmental Protection Agency, Addressing Uranium Contamination on the Navajo Nation. https://www3.epa.gov/region9/superfund/navajo-nation/index.html.

30 Barbara Rose Johnston, Susan E. Dawson and Gary E. Madsen, 'Uranium mining and milling: Navajo experiences in the American Southwest', in Barbara Rose Johnston, ed. *Half-lives and Half-truths: Confronting the Radioactive Legacies of the Cold War* (Santa Fe: School of Advanced Research Press, 2007), 98–100.

31 Johnston, Dawson and Madsen, 'Uranium mining and milling', 100; Voyles, *Wastelanding*, loc. 259.

32 Doug Brugge and Rob Goble, 'The History of Uranium Mining and the Navajo People', *American Journal of Public Health*, 92 (9), September 2002, 1411.

33 Ray C. Ringholz, *Uranium Frenzy: Saga of the Nuclear West* (Logan: Utah State University Press, 2002), Loc. 1088.

34 Johnston, Dawson and Madsen, 'Uranium mining and milling', 102; Ringholz, *Uranium Frenzy*, loc. 1005–13; Brugge and Goble, 'The History', 1414.

35 Brugge and Goble (p. 1412) explain a 'working level' of radon exposure as follows: 'Early measurements were of the concentration of radon in the air in mines – typically measured in picocuries per liter. Harley's work focused on the

radon daughters and led to the definition of a working level
as the measure of the energy released by radon daughters.
This provides a physical measure that is closely related to
the mechanism for biological damage. One working level is
a concentration of radon decay products that will release 1.3
million electron volts per liter of air. Depending on ventilation
and the amount of dust, a particular concentration of radon
in the air can correspond to different working levels. At
equilibrium (expected with poor ventilation), 1 working level
corresponds to 100 pCi/L in air.'

36 Johnston, Dawson and Madsen, 'Uranium mining and milling',
    105; Brugge and Goble, 'The History', 1413–14.
37 Brugge and Goble, 'The History', 1414; Johnston, Dawson and
    Madsen, 'Uranium mining and milling', 103; Carrie Arnold,
    'Once Upon a Mine: The Legacy of Uranium on the Navajo
    Nation', *Environmental Health Perspectives*, 122(2), February
    2014. http://ehp.niehs.nih.gov/122-a44/.
38 Judy Pasternak, 'A peril that dwelt among the Navajos', *The Los
    Angeles Times*, 19 November 2006. http://articles.latimes.com/
    print/2006/nov/19/nation/na-navajo19.
39 Doug Brugge, Jamie Delemos and Cat Bui, 'The Sequoyah
    Corporation Fuels Release and the Church Rock Spill:
    Unpublicized Nuclear Releases in American Indian
    Communities', *American Journal of Public Health*, 97(9), 2007,
    1597–8.
40 Pasternak, 'A peril that dwelt among the Navajos'; Judy
    Pasternak, 'Navajos' desert cleanup no more than a mirage',
    The Los Angeles Times, 21 November 2006. http://www.latimes.
    com/news/la-na-navajo21nov21-story.html.
41 Ringholz, *Uranium Frenzy*, loc. 544, 1821.
42 Bradford D. Cooley, 'The Navajo Uranium Ban: Tribal
    Sovereignty v. National Energy Demands', *Journal of Land,
    Resources, and Environmental Law*, 26(393), 2006, 3–4.
43 April Reese, 'Navajo Group to Take Uranium Mine Challenge
    to Human Rights Commission', *The New York Times*, 12 May,
    2011. http://www.nytimes.com/gwire/2011/05/12/12greenwire-
    navajo-group-to-take-uranium-mine-challenge-to-33718.
    html?pagewanted=all.
44 Anne Minard, 'Navajo Nation Slams Door on Deal That Would
    Have Allowed Uranium Mining', *Indian Country Today*,

1 August 2014. http://indiancountrytodaymedianetwork. com/2014/08/01/navajo-nation-slams-door-deal-would-have-allowed-uranium-mining-156143.

45 Graetz, 'Uranium Mining and First Peoples', 343.

46 Andrew Nikiforuk, 'Echoes of the Atomic Age: Cancer kills fourteen aboriginal uranium workers', *Calgary Herald*, 14 March 1998. Archived at: http://www.ccnr.org/deline_deaths.html.

47 Peter Blow, Dir. 'A Village of Widows', Lindum Films 1999. Timestamp 15:27

48 Ronald B. Barbour, 'Déline Dene Mining Tragedy', *First Nations Drum*, 22 December, 1998. http://www.firstnationsdrum. com/1998/12/deline-dene-mining-tragedy.

49 Sarah M. Gordon, 'Narratives Unearthed, or, How an Abandoned Mine Doesn't Really Abandon You', in Arn Keeling and John Sandlos, eds. *Mining and Communities in Northern Canada: History, Politics, and Memory* (University of Calgary Press, 2015), 64; Julie Salverson, 'They Never Told Us These Things', *Maisonneuve Quarterly*, 12 August, 2011. https:// maisonneuve.org/article/2011/08/12/they-never-told-us-these-things/.

50 Andrew Nikiforuk, 'Echoes of the Atomic Age: uranium haunts a northern aboriginal village', *Calgary Herald*, 14 March 1998, A4. Archived at: http://www.ccnr.org/deline_deaths.html.

51 Nikiforuk, 'Echoes of the Atomic Age'.

52 DÉLINE Dene Band Council, Call for Federal Response – 23 March 1998. Archived at: http://www.wise-uranium.org/ uippra.html#EXPINSUF.

53 Barbour, 'Déline Dene Mining Tragedy'.

54 Peter Blow, Dir. 'A Village of Widows', timestamp 29:00.

55 Peter C. Van Wyck, *The Highway of the Atom* (Montréal and Kingston: McGill-Queens University Press, 2010), loc. 225.

56 Nikiforuk, 'Echoes of the Atomic Age'; Van Wyck, *The Highway of the Atom*, loc. 695.

57 Van Wyck, *The Highway of the Atom*, loc. 781. The visit is also recorded in Peter Blow, Dir. 'A Village of Widows', timestamp 36.00–49.27.

58 WISE Uranium Project, Québec uranium mining moratorium. http://www.wise-uranium.org/uregcdn.html#CDNQCMOR; WISE Uranium Project, 'Matoush Project'. http://www.wise-uranium.org/upcdn.html#MATOUSH.

59 WISE Uranium Project, 'Nunavut'. http://www.wise-uranium.
    org/uregcdn.html#NU; Government of Nunavut Uranium
    Policy Statement. http://www.uranium.gov.nu.ca.

60 'Australia's Uranium', World Nuclear Association. http://
    www.world-nuclear.org/information-library/country-profiles/
    countries-a-f/australia.aspx.

61 'Indigenous people oppose Beverley uranium mine', *Green
    Left Weekly*, 24 March 1999. https://www.greenleft.org.au/
    node/19996; 'Uranium mine risks too great: Adnyamathanha
    Traditional Owner', *The Flinders News*, 21 August 2009.
    http://treatyrepublic.net/content/uranium-mine-risks-too-
    great-adnyamathanha-traditional-owner; 'Aboriginal people
    "not heard" over mine', 15 July 2009. http://www.abc.net.
    au/news/2009-07-15/aboriginal-people-not-heard-over-
    mine/1354254.

62 'Mining plan has SA Aborigines worried', *The World Today*,
    ABC Local Radio, 26 June 2008. Transcript at: http://www.abc.
    net.au/worldtoday/content/2008/s2286645.htm.

63 'Cameco's Yeelirrie uranium mine proposal knocked back in
    WA Goldfields', *ABC News Online*, 3 August 2016. http://www.
    abc.net.au/news/2016-08-03/uranium-mine-proposal-knocked-
    back-in-wa/7685538.

64 Environment, Communications, Information Technology and
    the Arts References Committee, *Regulating the Ranger, Jabiluka,
    Beverley and Honeymoon uranium mines* (Canberra: Australian
    Senate, October 2003), 22.

65 Environment, Communications, Information Technology and
    the Arts References Committee, *Jabiluka: The Undermining
    of Process*, Inquiry into the Jabiluka Uranium Mine Project
    (Canberra: Australian Senate, July 1999), 7.

66 *Jabiluka: The Undermining of Process*, 80.

67 Lauren Mellor, 'Rehabilitating Mirarr land: Uranium mining to
    end at Ranger?', *Chain Reaction*, No. 124, September 2015, 44.

68 Mellor, 'Rehabilitating Mirarr land', 46.

69 Gundjeihmi Aboriginal Corporation, 'Uranium Mining'. http://
    www.mirarr.net/uranium-mining.

70 *Regulating the Ranger, Jabiluka, Beverley and Honeymoon
    uranium mines*, 24–6, 289.

71 *Regulating the Ranger, Jabiluka, Beverley and Honeymoon
    uranium mines*, 46.

72 *Regulating the Ranger, Jabiluka, Beverley and Honeymoon uranium mines,* Appendix 6, 'Environmental incidents at Ranger', 289–303.

73 Tim Elliott, Ranger mine's uranium spill revealed to be Rio Tinto's second in a week, *The Sydney Morning Herald,* 11 December 2013. http://www.smh.com.au/national/ranger-mines-uranium-spill-revealed-to-be-rio-tintos-second-in-a-week-20131210-2z452.html.

74 Supervising scientist Report 207, *Investigation into the environmental impacts of the leach tank failure at Ranger uranium mine, December 2013.* Canberra: Department of Environment and Energy, 2014. https://www.environment.gov.au/node/37205.

75 *Regulating the Ranger, Jabiluka, Beverley and Honeymoon uranium mines,* xiii.

76 Liz Minchin and Lindsay Murdoch, 'Aboriginal cancer doubles near uranium mine', *The Age,* 23 November 2006. http://www.theage.com.au/news/national/aboriginal-cancer-doubles-near-uranium-mine/2006/11/22/1163871482163.html.

77 *Regulating the Ranger, Jabiluka, Beverley and Honeymoon uranium mines,* x–xiii; *Jabiluka: The Undermining of Process,* 58.

78 Ibid., xv.

79 Ibid., 77, 81.

80 Ibid., 4–5.

81 Ibid. 78.

82 'ERA signs long term Jabiluka agreement', *The Sydney Morning Herald,* 23 February 2005. http://www.smh.com.au/articles/2005/02/25/1109180077764.html.

83 Lindsay Murdoch, 'Owners speak out about Kakadu's uranium', *The Age,* 7 March 2006. http://www.theage.com.au/news/national/owners-speak-out-about-kakadus-uranium/2006/03/06/1141493611298.html; 'Rio's Jabiluka talk causes anger', *PM,* 23 May 2007. Transcript: http://www.abc.net.au/pm/content/2007/s1931353.htm.

84 Gundjeihmi Aboriginal Corporation, 'Uranium Mining'.

85 This figure is offered as a rough guide only and has been calculated by combining the 2015 total production of 71,343 tonnes U_3O_8 by \$40/lb – the spot price at the beginning of 2015 and the level at which uranium prices are expected to stabilize from 2018. Exact world total revenues are difficult to estimate,

because uranium is generally supplied against confidential long-term contracts (which however are estimated to be priced above spot prices at their lower levels). http://www.world-nuclear.org/information-library/nuclear-fuel-cycle/uranium-resources/uranium-markets.aspx.

86 *Managing Environmental and Health Impacts of Uranium Mining*, NEA No. 7062 (Paris, OECD, 2014).

5 Energy, Risk and Climate

1 James Hansen et al., 'Assessing "Dangerous Climate Change": Required Reduction of Carbon Emissions to Protect Young People, Future Generations and Nature', *PLoS ONE* 8(12) 2013: e81648.

2 Bill McKibben, 'Climate Deal: the Pistol has Fired, So Why Aren't We Running?', *Guardian*, 14 December 2015. http://www.theguardian.com/commentisfree/2015/dec/13/paris-climate-talks-15c-marathon-negotiating-physics.

3 John Nielson-Gammon, 'What Is Business As Usual?', *Climate Change National Forum*. 20 August 2014. http://climatechangenationalforum.org/what-is-business-as-usual/.

4 Malte Meinshausen, 'Paris climate targets aren't enough, but we can close the gap', *The Conversation*, 30 June 2016. https://theconversation.com/paris-climate-targets-arent-enough-but-we-can-close-the-gap-61798.

5 These figures include heating as well as electricity generation. Intergovernmental Panel on Climate Change, *Climate Change 2014: Synthesis Report*, 47.

6 Atoms for Peace, Address by Mr. Dwight D. Eisenhower, President of the United States of America, to the 470th Plenary Meeting of the United Nations General Assembly, 8 December 1953. https://www.iaea.org/about/history/atoms-for-peace-speech.

7 The Treaty on the Non-Proliferation of Nuclear Weapons, http://www.un.org/en/conf/npt/2005/npttreaty.html.

8 Nuclear Energy Agency and Organization for Economic Co-Operation and Development, *Nuclear Energy and the Kyoto Protocol* (Paris: OECD, 2002), 8.

9 World Nuclear Association, *World Nuclear Power Reactors &*

Uranium Requirements, 10 August 2016. http://www.world-nuclear.org/information-library/facts-and-figures/world-nuclear-power-reactors-and-uranium-requireme.aspx.

10 International Atomic Energy Agency, *Climate Change and Nuclear Power 2015*. http://www-pub.iaea.org/books/IAEABooks/10928/Climate-Change-and-Nuclear-Power-2015; 'World Nuclear Association at COP 21'. http://www.world-nuclear.org/focus/climate-change-and-nuclear-energy/cop21.aspx.

11 IAEA, *Climate Change and Nuclear Power*, 80–3.

12 Ibid., 23, 34.

13 Pornrapeepat Bhasaputra, Vivat Chutiprapat and Woraratana Pattaraprakorn, 'The Successive Development of Nuclear Energy in the World', *GMSARN International Journal*, 5(2), 2011, 128.

14 *Nuclear for Climate Position Paper*, 3; IAEA, *Climate Change and Nuclear Power*, 25.

15 IAEA, *Climate Change and Nuclear Power*, Foreword, 13–16.

16 World Nuclear Association, 'Nuclear Power in the United Kingdom', 10 August 2016. http://www.world-nuclear.org/information-library/country-profiles/countries-t-z/united-kingdom.aspx; Damian Carrington, 'China to take one-third stake in £24bn Hinkley nuclear power station', *Guardian*, 20 October 2015. https://www.theguardian.com/environment/2015/oct/20/china-to-take-one-third-stake-in-24bn-hinkley-nuclear-power-station.

17 Terry Macalister, 'Hinkley Point C may cost £30bn in "top-up payments", warns watchdog', *Guardian*, 13 July 2016. https://www.theguardian.com/uk-news/2016/jul/13/hinkley-point-c-cost-30bn-top-up-payments-nao-report.

18 Peter Walker and Ewen MacAskill, 'Chinese-built reactor at Bradwell could have "major impact" on estuary', *Guardian*, 19 October 2015. https://www.theguardian.com/environment/2015/oct/19/chinese-built-reactor-bradwell-impact-essex-estuary-plant-nuclear.

19 Rowena Mason and Frances Perraudin, 'Nuclear deals with China could endanger UK national security, says Labour', *Guardian*, 16 October 2015. https://www.theguardian.com/environment/2015/oct/16/nuclear-deals-with-china-could-endanger-uk-national-security-says-labour.

20   Emily Gosden, 'UK new nuclear plan will fail without private investors, says Horizon chief', *The Telegraph*, 14 February 2016. http://www.telegraph.co.uk/finance/newsbysector/ energy/12156773/UK-new-nuclear-plan-will-fail-without-private-investors-says-Horizon-chief.html.

21   Howard Johns, 'The government seems intent on ending the solar power industry. It's madness', *Guardian*, 18 October 2015. https://www.theguardian.com/commentisfree/2015/oct/18/ southern-solar-power-industry-company; Emma Howard, 'Revealed: Many more solar firms face closure if government cuts go ahead', *Guardian*, 19 October 2015. https://www. theguardian.com/environment/2015/oct/19/revealed-many-more-solar-firms-face-closure-if-government-cuts-go-ahead.

22   Jeff Kingston, 'Mismanaging risk and the Fukushima nuclear crisis', in Paul Bacon and Christopher Hobson eds. *Human Security and Japan's Triple Disaster* (London and New York: Routledge, 2014), 57.

23   David Schlissel, Michael Mullett and Robert Alvarez, *Nuclear Loan Guarantees: Another Taxpayer Bailout Ahead?* (Cambridge MA: Union of Concerned Scientists, March 2009), 2.

24   Jessica R. Lovering, Arthur Yip, Ted Nordhaus, 'Historical construction costs of global nuclear power reactors', *Energy Policy*, 91, 2016, 379.

25   Debbie Carlson, 'This new technology could save the troubled nuclear power industry', *Guardian*, 17 October 2016. https:// www.theguardian.com/sustainable-business/2016/oct/16/ safer-small-nuclear-reactors-power-plant-technology?CMP= twt_gu.

26   World Nuclear Association, 'Radioactive Waste Management'. July 2016. http://www.world-nuclear.org/information-library/nuclear-fuel-cycle/nuclear-wastes/radioactive-waste-management.aspx. See also *Spent Fuel Reprocessing Options*, IAEA-TECDOC-1587 (Vienna: International Atomic Energy Agency, 2008), 2.

27   *Strategy for the Management and Disposal of Used Nuclear Fuel and High-Level Radioactive Waste* (United States: Department of Energy, January 2013), 3.

28   Rodney C. Ewing, 'Nuclear waste forms for actinides', *PNAS*, 96(7), March 1999. http://www.pnas.org/content/96/7/3432.

29   United States Nuclear Regulatory Commission. 'Backgrounder

on Radioactive Waste'. http://www.nrc.gov/reading-rm/doc-collections/fact-sheets/radwaste.html.

30 Canadian Nuclear Safety Commission, 'High-level radioactive waste', http://nuclearsafety.gc.ca/eng/waste/high-level-waste/index.cfm

31 *Spent Fuel Reprocessing Options*, IAEA-TECDOC-1587 (Vienna: International Atomic Energy Agency, 2008), 2, 51–2; Union of Concerned Scientists, 'Nuclear Reprocessing: Dangerous Dirty and Expensive'. http://www.ucsusa.org/nuclear-power/nuclear-plant-security/nuclear-reprocessing#.V72crPkrLng.

32 International Atomic Energy Agency, 'The Joint Convention'. http://www-ns.iaea.org/conventions/waste-jointconvention.asp?s=6&l=40.

33 *Safety and Security of Commercial Spent Nuclear Fuel Storage,* Public Report (National Academies Press, 2006). http://www.nap.edu/catalog/11263/safety-and-security-of-commercial-spent-nuclear-fuel-storage-public; Patrick Malone and R. Jeffrey Smith, 'Scientists say nuclear fuel pools around the country pose safety and health risks', *Centre for Public Integrity*, 20 May, 2016. https://www.publicintegrity.org/2016/05/20/19712/scientists-say-nuclear-fuel-pools-around-country-pose-safety-and-health-risks.

34 *Strategy for the Management and Disposal of Used Nuclear Fuel and High-Level Radioactive Waste* (United States: Department of Energy, January 2013), 2.

35 Nuclear Waste Management Organization, *Choosing a Way Forward: the Future Management of Canada's Used Nuclear Fuel.* https://www.nwmo.ca/~/media/Site/Reports/2015/11/11/06/53/342_NWMO_Final_Study_Summary_E.ashx?la=en.

36 Declan Butler, 'France digs deep for nuclear waste', *Nature* 466, 804 – 805, 13 August 2010.

37 Nuclear Fuel Cycle Royal Commission Report, May 2016 (Government of South Australia, 2016). http://nuclearrc.sa.gov.au/.

38 *The Long Term Storage Of Radioactive Waste: Safety And Sustainability,* A Position Paper Of International Experts (Vienna: International Atomic Energy Agency, 2003).

39 'The Chances of Another Chernobyl Before 2050? 50%, Say

Safety Specialists', *MIT Technology Review*, 17 April 2015. https://www.technologyreview.com/s/536886/the-chances-of-another-chernobyl-before-2050-50-say-safety-specialists/.

40 IAEA and OECD, *INES: The International Nuclear and Radiological Events Scale*. https://www.iaea.org/sites/default/files/ines.pdf.

41 'Nuclear power plant accidents: listed and ranked since 1952', *Guardian*. https://www.theguardian.com/news/datablog/2011/mar/14/nuclear-power-plant-accidents-list-rank accessed 30 June 2016.

42 Charpak and Garwin, *From Megawatts to Megatons*, 172–4.

43 Nuclear Energy Agency, *Chernobyl: Assessment of Radiological and Health Impact*, Chapter 1: the Site and Accident Sequence. https://www.oecd-nea.org/rp/chernobyl/c01.html.

44 Nuclear Energy Agency, *Chernobyl: Assessment of Radiological and Health Impact*.

45 Charpak and Garwin, *From Megawatts to Megatons*, 190.

46 United Nations Scientific Committee on the Effects of Atomic Radiation, *The Chernobyl Accident: UNSCEAR's Assessments of the Radiation Effects*. http://www.unscear.org/unscear/en/chernobyl.html; Charpak and Garwin, *From Megawatts to Megatons*, 189.

47 Nuclear Energy Agency, *Chernobyl: Assessment of Radiological and Health Impact*, Chapter 3: Reactions of National Authorities. https://www.oecd-nea.org/rp/chernobyl/c03.html.

48 The Chernobyl Forum, *Chernobyl's Legacy: Health, Environmental and Socio-Economic Impacts and Recommendations to the Governments of Belarus, the Russian Federation and Ukraine*, Second Revised Version, 2003–2005, 33–4. https://www.iaea.org/sites/default/files/chernobyl.pdf.

49 World Nuclear Association, 'Fukushima: Background on Reactors', http://www.world-nuclear.org/information-library/safety-and-security/safety-of-plants/appendices/fukushima-reactor-background.aspx; Richard Broinowski, *Fallout from Fukushima* (Melbourne, Scribe, 2012), 11–12.

50 Becky Oskin, Japan Earthquake & Tsunami of 2011: Facts and Information, LiveScience, http://www.livescience.com/39110-japan-2011-earthquake-tsunami-facts.html.

51 Kenji E. Kushida, 'Japan's Fukushima Nuclear Disaster: an Overview ', in Edward D. Blandford and Scott D. Sagan eds.

Learning from a Disaster: Improving Nuclear Safety and Security after Fukushima (Stanford: Stanford University Press, 2016), 23.

52 Independent Investigation Commission on the Fukushima Nuclear Accident, *The Fukushima Daiichi Nuclear Power Station Disaster* (London and New York: Routledge 2014), 4.

53 Broinowski, *Fallout from Fukushima*, 14–15; World Nuclear Association, 'Fukushima Accident', http://www.world-nuclear. org/information-library/safety-and-security/safety-of-plants/ fukushima-accident.aspx.

54 Kushida, 'Japan's Fukushima Nuclear Disaster: an Overview', 20.

55 'Lessons of the Fukushima Daiichi nuclear power station accident on the quest for resilience', in Independent Investigation Commission on the Fukushima Nuclear Accident, *The Fukushima Daiichi Nuclear Power Station Disaster* (London and New York: Routledge 2014), 177.

56 'Impact of radioactive material released into the environment', in Independent Investigation Commission on the Fukushima Nuclear Accident, *The Fukushima Daiichi Nuclear Power Station Disaster* (London and New York: Routledge 2014), 125.

57 Kingston, 'Mismanaging risk and the Fukushima nuclear crisis', 50–1; Justin McCurry, 'Fukushima disaster could have been avoided, nuclear plant operator admits', *Guardian*, 15 October 2012. https://www.theguardian.com/ environment/2012/oct/15/fukushima-disaster-avoided-nuclear-plant.

58 Kushida, 'Japan's Fukushima Nuclear Disaster: an Overview', 12, 22.

59 'Letter from Koichi Kitazawa, Chairman of the Independent Investigation Commission on the Fukushima Nuclear Accident', in Independent Investigation Commission on the Fukushima Nuclear Accident, *The Fukushima Daiichi Nuclear Power Station Disaster* (London and New York: Routledge 2014), loc. 111.

60 Broinowski, *Fallout from Fukushima*, 17–18.

61 United Nations Scientific Committee on the Effects of Atomic Radiation, Sources, Effects And Risks Of Ionizing Radiation UNSCEAR 2013 Report to the General Assembly with Scientific Annexes VOLUME I Scientific Annex A (New York: United Nations, 2014), 9–10. Http://www.unscear.org/docs/ publications/2013/UNSCEAR_2013_GA-Report.pdf.

62 Paul Bacon and Christopher Hobson eds. *Human Security and Japan's Triple Disaster* (London and New York: Routledge, 2014), 8–9; 'Fukushima's appalling death toll', *The Japan Times*, 1 March 2014, and 'Death toll grows in 3/11 aftermath', *The Japan Times*, 15 March 2015. http://www.japantimes.co.jp/news/2015/03/15/national/death-toll-grows-in-311-aftermath/#.V7x7avkrKsq.

63 Bacon and Hobson eds. *Human Security and Japan's Triple Disaster*, 8; 'Fukushima disaster bill more than $105bn', double earlier estimate – study, *RT News*. 27 Aug, 2014. https://www.rt.com/news/183052-japan-fukushima-costs-study/.

64 World Nuclear Association, 'Safety of Nuclear Power Reactors', May 2016. http://www.world-nuclear.org/information-library/safety-and-security/safety-of-plants/safety-of-nuclear-power-reactors.aspx.

65 'Letter from Koichi Kitazawa', loc. 153.

66 Ibid., loc. 171, 183; Kingston, 'Mismanaging risk and the Fukushima nuclear crisis', 45.

67 'Letter from Koichi Kitazawa', loc. 131.

68 'EDITORIAL: Extending life of Mihama nuclear reactor raises doubts on safety', *The Asahi Shimbun*, 8 August, 2016. http://www.asahi.com/ajw/articles/AJ201608080025.html.

69 Kingston, 'Mismanaging risk and the Fukushima nuclear crisis', 43.

70 'Convention on Nuclear Safety', https://www-ns.iaea.org/conventions/nuclear-safety.asp?s=6&l=41.

71 Vienna Declaration on Nuclear Safety. https://www.iaea.org/sites/default/files/cns_viennadeclaration090215.pdf.

72 IAEA, 'Enhancing Radiation Safety: IAEA Signs Two Practical Arrangements with Russian Regulatory Authorities', 25 July 2016. https://www.iaea.org/newscenter/news/enhancing-radiation-safety-iaea-signs-two-practical-arrangements-with-russian-regulatory-authorities; 'IAEA Mission: Kenya Committed to Radiation Safety, Needs to Ensure Regulatory Body's Independence', 20 July 2016. https://www.iaea.org/newscenter/pressreleases/iaea-mission-kenya-committed-to-radiation-safety-needs-to-ensure-regulatory-bodys-independence.

73 'Convention on Nuclear Safety'.

74 IAEA, 'Guidelines regarding the Review Process under

the Convention on Nuclear Safety', Information Circular
INFIRC/571/Rev.7, 16 January 2015. https://www.iaea.org/
sites/default/files/infcirc57117_0.pdf.

75 Gerrit Wiesmann, 'Siemens drops Rosatom nuclear plant
ambitions', *Financial Times*, September 18, 2011. http://www.
ft.com/cms/s/0/2e711fde-e1e9-11e0-9915-00144feabdc0.
html#axzz4ILa9WQsO; Deborah Cole, 'Fukushima fallout:
Germany abandons nuclear energy', *The Sydney Morning Herald*,
31 May 2011. http://www.smh.com.au/world/fukushima-
fallout-germany-abandons-nuclear-energy-20110530-1fczb.html;
Charles Digges, 'Siemens abandons nuclear power, focusing
on renewables and leaving Rosatom joint venture dangling',
Bellona, 20 September 2011. http://bellona.org/news/nuclear-
issues/2011-09-siemens-abandons-nuclear-power-focusing-on-
renewables-and-leaving-rosatom-joint-venture-dangling.

76 IDN, 'Nuclear Industry Upbeat Despite Fukushima – Analysis',
Eurasia Review, 11 March, 2012. http://www.eurasiareview.
com/11032012-nuclear-industry-upbeat-despite-fukushima-
analysis/

6 CHALLENGES AND FUTURES

1 Anthony Burke, 'Nuclear futures after the #NPT2015', *Security
Dilemmas*, 3 June 2015. https://securitydilemmas.wordpress.
com/2015/06/03/nuclear-futures-after-the-npt2015/; William
C. Potter, 'The Unfulfilled Promise of the 2015 NPT Review
Conference', *Survival*, 58(1), 2016, 151–78; Cesar Jaramillo,
'NPT Review Conference: No outcome document better than a
weak one', *Bulletin of the Atomic Scientists*, 3 June 2015.

2 Bureau of International Security and Nonproliferation, 'Article
X of the Nuclear Nonproliferation Treaty: Deterring and
Responding to Withdrawal by Treaty Violators', 2 February
2007. http://2001-2009.state.gov/t/isn/rls/other/80518.htm.

3 Travis Wheeler, 'China's MIRVs: Separating Fact From Fiction',
The Diplomat, 18 May 2016. http://thediplomat.com/2016/05/
chinas-mirvs-separating-fact-from-fiction/.

4 Secretary-General's message to the Opening Plenary of the
Treaty on the Non-Proliferation of Nuclear Weapons [delivered
by the Deputy Secretary-General Jan Eliasson], New York,

27 April 2015. http://www.un.org/sg/statements/index.
asp?nid=8581.

5 For detail about the agreement between Iran and the P5+1
   see http://www.state.gov/p/nea/p5/; Kenneth Katzman, *Iran
   Sanctions*, 7-5700, RS20871 (Washington DC: Congressional
   Research Service, 18 May 2016). https://www.fas.org/sgp/crs/
   mideast/RS20871.pdf.

6 Taylor Kate Brown, '25 years on at America's most
   contaminated nuclear waste site', *BBC News*, 11 June 2014.
   http://www.bbc.co.uk/news/magazine-26658719; Robin
   McKie, 'Sellafield: the most hazardous place in Europe', *The
   Observer*, 19 April 2009. https://www.theguardian.com/
   environment/2009/apr/19/sellafield-nuclear-plant-cumbria-
   hazards.

7 Arms Control Association. 'Nuclear Weapons: Who Has
   What at a Glance'. https://www.armscontrol.org/factsheets/
   Nuclearweaponswhohaswhat. The US and Russia numbers
   reflect progress towards implementation of the New START
   Treaty, under which they will reduce to 'aggregate limits' of
   1550 strategic warheads on 700 deployed launch platforms (air,
   sea or missile). These limits must be reached by 5 February
   2018 and the treaty is only in force until 2021. http://www.state.
   gov/t/avc/newstart/index.htm.

8 Simond de Galbert, 'President Hollande's Message on Nuclear
   Deterrence', *CSIS Commentary*, 9 March 2015 (Washington DC:
   Centre for Strategic and International Studies). https://www.
   csis.org/analysis/president-hollande%E2%80%99s-message-
   nuclear-deterrence.

9 'A guide to Trident and the debate about replacement',
   BBC News, 18 July 2016. http://www.bbc.co.uk/news/uk-
   politics-13442735; Rowena Mason and Anushka Asthana,
   'Commons votes for Trident renewal by majority of 355',
   Guardian, 18 July 2016. https://www.theguardian.com/
   uk-news/2016/jul/18/mps-vote-in-favour-of-trident-renewal-
   nuclear-deterrent.

10 'David Cameron: Jeremy Corbyn is a risk to national security
   and will take Britain back the 1970s-PMQs live', *The Telegraph*.
   http://www.telegraph.co.uk/news/politics/pmqs/12110164/
   David-Cameron-Jeremy-Corbyn-is-a-risk-to-national-security-
   and-will-take-Britain-back-the-1970s-PMQs-live.html; Greg

Heffer, 'May's first victory: Parliament votes to renew Trident amid splits in the Labour party', *The Express*, 19 July 2016. http://www.express.co.uk/news/politics/690665/Trident-debate-Theresa-May-Jeremy-Corbyn-Labour-splits-nuclear-weapons-vote-David-Cameron.

11 Nuclear Threat Initiative, Country Information. http://www. nti.org/analysis/articles/china-nuclear-disarmament/ http:// www.nti.org/analysis/articles/india-nuclear-disarmament/; Frank O'Donnell, 'India and Pakistan in 2013: Nuclear Extroversion, Political Introversion', *European Leadership Network*, 4 June 2013. http://www.europeanleadershipnetwork. org/india-and-pakistan-in-2013-nuclear-extroversion-political-introversion_612.html.

12 2010 Review Conference of the Parties to the Treaty on the Non-Proliferation of Nuclear Weapons, *Final Document: Volume I*, PT/CONF.2010/50 (New York: United Nations, 2010), 20–1.

13 Gareth Evans, Tanya Ogilvie-White and Ramesh Thakur, *Nuclear Weapons: The State of Play 2015* (Canberra: Centre For Nuclear Non-Proliferation And Disarmament, 2015), xiii–xiv.

14 Reaching Critical Will, 'Humanitarian impact of nuclear weapons'. http://www.reachingcriticalwill.org/disarmament-fora/hinw.

15 Anthony Burke, 'Nuclear futures after the #NPT2015', *Security Dilemmas*, 3 June 2015. https://securitydilemmas.wordpress. com/2015/06/03/nuclear-futures-after-the-npt2015/.

16 'Humanitarian pledge for the prohibition and elimination of nuclear weapons', Resolution 70/48 adopted by the General Assembly on 7 December 2015, 15-16802 (E) [on the report of the First Committee (A/70/460)].

17 United Nations Office at Geneva, Taking Forward Multi-lateral Nuclear Disarmament Negotiations. http://www.unog.ch/ oewg-ndn; 'Report of the Open-ended Working Group Taking Forward Multi-lateral Nuclear Disarmament Negotiations', Advanced copy, paras. 33–9.

18 Dr Thomas Hajnoczi, Permanent Representative of Austria to the United Nations, Geneva, 31 August 2016. Interview with author.

19 Yury Yudin, *Multilateralisation Of The Nuclear Fuel Cycle: Assessing The Existing Proposals* (Geneva: United Nations Institute of Disarmament Research, 2009).

20 George Perkovitch and James M. Acton, *Abolishing Nuclear Weapons*, Adelphi Paper 396 (London and New York: IISS and Routledge, 2008), 90–91.

21 *Fissile Material (Cutoff) Treaty: Background and overview of recent literature* (London and Washington: British American Security Information Council, 2013).

22 2010 Review Conference of the Parties, *Final Document: Volume I*, para. 6, 3.

23 Gareth Evans and Yoriko Kawaguchi, *Eliminating Nuclear Threats: A Practical Agenda for Global Policymakers* (Canberra and Tokyo: International Commission on Nuclear Non-proliferation and Disarmament, 2009), xvii.

24 2010 Review Conference of the Parties, *Final Document: Volume I*, para. 79, 12.

25 Evans and Kawaguchi, *Eliminating Nuclear Threats*, 187, 205.

26 George Perkovitch and James M. Acton, *Abolishing Nuclear Weapons*, Adelphi Paper 396 (London and New York: IISS and Routledge, 2008); David Cortwright and Raimo Väyrynen, *Towards Nuclear Zero*, Adelphi Paper 410 (London: IISS and Routledge, 2010); James M. Acton, *Deterrence During Disarmament: Deep Nuclear Reductions and International Security*, Adelphi Paper 417 (London and New York: IISS and Routledge, 2010). See also George Perkovich and Patricia Lewis, 'The Vantage Point', Research paper commissioned by the International Commission on Nuclear Non-proliferation and Disarmament, January 2009.

27 George Perkovitch and James M. Acton, eds. *Abolishing Nuclear Weapons: A Debate* (Carnegie Endowment for International Peace, 2009); James M. Acton, *Low Numbers: A Practical Path to Deep Nuclear Reductions* (Washington DC: Carnegie Endowment for International Peace, 2011).

28 Evans and Kawaguchi, *Eliminating Nuclear Threats*.

29 Perkovitch and Acton, *Abolishing Nuclear Weapons*, 55–69; Campbell Craig, 'The Resurgent Idea of World Government', *Ethics & International Affairs*, 22(02), Summer 2008, 133–42.

30 Cortwright and Väyrynen, *Towards Nuclear Zero*, 148–58.

31 This problem is the central theme of Acton, *Deterrence During Disarmament* and Lawrence Freedman's chapter in

Perkovitch and Acton, *Abolishing Nuclear Weapons: A Debate*, 141–5.

32 Evans and Kawaguchi, *Eliminating Nuclear Threats*, 187, 205.

33 Perkovitch and Acton, *Abolishing Nuclear Weapons*, 23.

34 Ibid., 54.

Selected Readings

There is a large body of relevant literature that covers the various facets of the atomic age. Interested readers can mine this book's endnotes for specific sources, particularly for reports or research papers. Here I will list some book-length studies. Good introductions to the science include Jeremy Bernstein, *Plutonium: A History of the World's Most Dangerous Element* (Sydney: NewSouth and Cornell University Press, 2009) and Richard L. Garwin and Georges Charpak, *Megawatts and Megatons: The Future of Nuclear Power and Nuclear Weapons* (Chicago: University of Chicago Press, 2002) and a general treatment of the uranium story is provided by Tom Zoellner, *Uranium: War, Energy and the Rock that Shaped the World* (London: Viking, 2009).

Three important overviews of the global nuclear order and NPT regime include William Walker, *A Perpetual Menace: Nuclear Weapons and International Order* (London and New York: Routledge, 2010), Maria Rost Rublee, *Nonproliferation Norms: Why States Choose Nuclear Restraint* (Athens, GA: University of Georgia Press, 2009) and Shampa Biswas, *Nuclear Desire: Power and the Postcolonial Nuclear Order* (Minneapolis and London: University of Minnesota Press, 2014). Contemporary treatments of non-proliferation and disarmament issues include Mark Fitzpatrick, *Overcoming Pakistan's Nuclear Dangers* (London and New York: IISS and Routledge, 2014), Gareth Evans and Yoriko Kawaguchi, *Eliminating Nuclear Threats: A Practical Agenda for Global*

Policymakers (Canberra and Tokyo: International Commission on Nuclear Non-proliferation and Disarmament, 2009), George Perkovitch and James M. Acton, eds. *Abolishing Nuclear Weapons: A Debate* (Carnegie Endowment for International Peace, 2009) and the classic strategic history is Lawrence Freedman, *The Evolution of Nuclear Strategy*, 3rd edn (Basingstoke: Palgrave Macmillan, 2003). A recent treatment of nuclear weapons and risk is Patricia Lewis, Heather Williams, Benoît Pelopidas and Sasan Aghlani, *Too Close for Comfort: Cases of Near Nuclear Use and Options for Policy* (London: Chatham House, April 2014) and a truly eye-popping story about nuclear safety during the Cold War is Eric Schlosser, *Command and Control* (London and New York: Penguin, 2014).

A moving and exhaustively researched account of the use of nuclear weapons is Paul Ham, *Hiroshima and Nagasaki: The Real Story of the Atomic Bombings and their Aftermath* (London: Doubleday, 2012) and a critical analysis of the geo-politics behind the decision can be found in Gar Alperovitz, *The Decision to Use the Atomic Bomb and the Architecture of an American Myth* (Knopf, 1995). Essays by the scientific direc-tor of the Manhattan Project are in J. Robert Oppenheimer, *Uncommon Sense* (Boston: Birkhauser, 1984) and an excellent political and scientific biography of Oppenheimer was writ-ten by Kai Bird and Martin Sherwin, *American Prometheus* (New York: Atlantic Books, 2009). A few historical accounts make for fascinating and tragic reading: David Holloway, *Stalin and the Bomb* (New Haven and London: Yale University Press, 1994) is an exhaustive exploration of the Soviet nuclear programme and Gerard J. DeGroot, *The Bomb: A Life* (Cambridge, MA: Harvard University Press, 2004) an acces-sible history. Richard Rhodes has authored two significant histories of the development of nuclear weapons, *The Making of the Atomic Bomb* (New York and London: Simon and

Schuster, 2012) and *Dark Sun: The Making of the Hydrogen Bomb* (New York and London: Simon and Schuster, 1995). One account by a former Kennedy administration official and nuclear insider is McGeorge Bundy, *Danger And Survival: Choices About The Bomb In The First Fifty Years* (New York: Vintage, 1988). Another nuclear insider who was central to US decision-making during the Cuban missile crisis records his thoughts in Robert S. McNamara and James G. Blight, *Wilson's Ghost* (New York: Public Affairs, 2003), which is a kind of companion volume to the Errol Morris film *The Fog of War*.

There are relatively few long treatments of uranium mining issues and those tend to come from anthropology and sociology, such as Barbara Rose Johnston, ed. *Half-lives and Half-truths: Confronting the Radioactive Legacies of the Cold War* (Santa Fe: School of Advanced Research Press, 2007), Arn Keeling and John Sandlos, *Mining and Communities in Northern Canada* (University of Calgary Press, 2015) and Stephanie Malin, *The Price of Nuclear Power: Uranium Communities and Environmental Justice* (New Brunswick: Rutgers University Press, 2015). Two remarkable texts from the environmental humanities respectively explore the experiences of the Navajo and the Dené: Traci Brynne Voyles, *Wastelanding: Legacies of Uranium Mining in Navajo Country* (Minneapolis and London: University of Minnesota Press, 2015) and Peter C. Van Wyck, *The Highway of the Atom* (Montréal and Kingston: McGill-Queens University Press, 2010).

A valuable multi-sided analysis of the Fukushima disaster can be found in Paul Bacon and Christopher Hobson eds. *Human Security and Japan's Triple Disaster* (London and New York: Routledge, 2014) and many personal stories are also collected in Richard Broinowski, *Fallout from Fukushima* (Melbourne: Scribe, 2012). The definitive report on the events is contained in Independent Investigation Commission on the Fukushima Nuclear Accident, *The Fukushima Daiichi Nuclear Power Station Disaster* (London and New York: Routledge 2014).

Index